BSP PRACTICAL GUIDES

YOU ARE THE GOVERNOR

How to be Effective in Your Local School

Barbara Bullivant has been a school governor for more than eighteen years, in primary, secondary and special schools, and has chaired three governing bodies. She has been an honorary secretary of the Confederation for the Advancement of State Education, a council member of the Advisory Centre for Education, and a member of the executive committee of the National Children's Bureau. She is currently honorary secretary of the National Association of Governors and Managers, and also of the Home and School Council.

She is married to the headteacher of a northern comprehensive school, and has four sons, all of whom are involved with education.

GW00713237

You Are the Governor

How To Be Effective in Your Local School

Illustrations by Nigel Paige

Barbara Bullivant

Bedford Square Press

Published by
BEDFORD SQUARE PRESS
of the
National Council for Voluntary Organisations
26 Bedford Square, London WC1 3HU

First published 1988
Text copyright © Barbara Bullivant 1988
Illustrations copyright © Nigel Paige 1988

ISBN 0 7199 1233 4

Typeset set by AKM Associates (UK) Ltd, Southall, London

Printed and bound in England by J.W. Arrowsmith Ltd, Bristol

British Library Cataloguing in Publication Data

Bullivant, Barbara
    You are the governor: how to be effective
    in your local school. – (Practical guides).
    1. Great Britain. Schools. Governors. Role.
    I. Title   II. Series
    379.1′531′0941

ISBN 0-7199-1233-4

Contents

Introduction

Many people are now school governors who have not previously been involved with the education service in this way. They are motivated by a desire to serve the school, the community and the children, but may feel in need of help.

If you are one of these governors, this book is designed to help you to find out what your powers and duties are, where you fit into the system, and how you can be effective. There has been much new legislation in recent years, giving a new role to school governors,

and there will be more changes in the future. Although some of the decisions may seem to be controversial, and may worry new governors, information helps to take away the mystery, explain the complex issues involved, and enable you to reach sensible decisions.

This book covers the school system in England and Wales. Scotland and Northern Ireland do not at present have a similar system, although schemes to involve parents and the community in running schools are under consideration.

The book was completed as the 1988 Education Act received the royal assent. The issues which were debated both inside and outside Parliament are covered in the relevant sections of the book. Where the timetable for implementing sections of the Act is known, the relevant dates have been included.

1
The System

Not all schools have identical arrangements for governing. This first chapter looks at where different kinds of schools fit into the system.

Boards of governors

In Britain, there is a long tradition of appointing groups of lay people to oversee the provision of services to the community which involve the spending of public money. Those involved do not usually do any of the work of the service, but they may decide on the level of service to be provided, who shall do the work, and the general policies involved. They will also look at how well the policies have been carried out, and consider how to deal with any problems which arise. Such people are often referred to as 'boards of governors' or 'governing bodies'. They exist in many areas of life: theatres and sports may have their boards of governors, as do independent institutions.

The 1944 Education Act said that all maintained schools should have a body, although it permitted schools to be grouped together for the purpose of governing. Different types of schools have different arrangements for governing. The type and size of the school affects many aspects of its organisation, such as the number of teachers, the amount of money available to run the school, and the size and composition of its governing body.

Schools which are financed by public money (rates and taxes) are 'maintained' schools, and fall into various categories.

County schools

These are the schools which are owned and run by a local education authority (LEA), which will be either a shire county, a metropolitan borough or a London borough. The schools are divided into primary and secondary, although within these categories the schools may have other names. A primary school may be infant, first, junior or middle, if the children are between the ages of 5 and 12. Some primary schools may have younger children, but the LEA does not have to provide for all children under 5, and parents do not have to send their children to school until they are 5. Virtually all primary schools are mixed.

A secondary school may be called comprehensive, modern, technical, grammar, high or middle. Middle schools in the secondary sector, rather than the primary, have children who stay until they are 13 or 14. The schools may be mixed or single sex.

Some schools, both primary and secondary, may have extra community facilities, such as a clinic, library, youth club, adult education centre, sports centre and so on, and may be called community schools or campuses. Governors of these schools will have extra responsiblities.

Special schools are provided by the LEA for children who have special needs, which cannot be met in ordinary, 'mainstream' schools. These schools may be primary or secondary, and may cater for children who have a mental or physical disability, or emotional problems. Some non-maintained special schools are also used by local authorities, who may have some involvement in the governing of the school.

Voluntary schools

These schools are run jointly by the LEA and another body, usually a church foundation. They are a continuing acknowledgement of the fact that the churches provided much of the education which was available in England and Wales before 1870. In addition to the primary/secondary division, these schools are of three types:

CONTROLLED SCHOOLS
The LEA provides all the costs involved in the running and management of the schools, and the number of LEA-appointed governors exceeds the number appointed by the foundation.

AIDED SCHOOLS
While the LEA provides most of the costs in connection with these

schools, the foundation has to meet some expenses. Foundation governors outnumber the LEA governors. The governors have wider powers than in other maintained schools.

SPECIAL AGREEMENT SCHOOLS

At the time when the present system was set up, some schools had trust deeds which required special arrangements to be made for their governing.

2
Who Are the Governors?

This chapter looks at who governors are, how the present numbers and types of governors were decided on, the legal setting, and the present composition of boards for different types and sizes of school.

Governors since 1944

Although the 1944 Education Act established that all schools should have a board of governors, in many cities all the primary schools were grouped together and governed by a sub-committee of the education committee, while secondary schools were often governed in groups of seven or eight schools. All the governors were elected councillors, who had many other commitments and were not able to give the time to get to know the schools.

By 1965, parents and others were beginning to seek changes to the system, which gave them no say. In 1975 the government appointed a committee under the chairmanship of Tom Taylor 'to review the arrangements for . . . the government of maintained primary and secondary schools in England and Wales'. The Committee's Report *A New Partnership for Our Schools* (1977), also called the Taylor Report, recommended that each school should have a governing body comprising four equal groups of governors: those appointed by the LEA, those elected by parents, those elected by school staff, and those from the community who would be co-opted by the other governors. The report also made recommendations about what such a body should do.

The 1980 Education Act did not go as far as the report recommended, but did give teachers and parents the right to elect their representatives to the board, and ensured that, eventually, every school would have its own board.

Some LEAs had been moving ahead during the 1970s, and making places available for parents, teachers and others. The pioneer was Sheffield where, from 1970, separate boards were established for all mainstream schools (special schools came later). Each board had places for LEA nominees, elected parents, teachers and non-teaching staff, elected pupils in secondary schools, and many community representatives, including those from higher education and the business community.

The 1986 Education Act

In 1986 another Education Act was passed, which provided for an increase in the minimum number of parent governors, and laid new duties on the boards. The full implementation of this Act in September 1988 means that non-teaching staff cannot have a place by right on the board, and that no one under 18 may be a governor, thus removing pupil governors from those schools where they formerly had a place. All boards will have some co-optative places, and governors must consider whether the local business community is adequately represented on the board, and if not, use some of the co-optative places to remedy this deficiency.

Primary schools in those areas where there is a 'minor authority' – a town or parish council – must retain a place on the governing body for a representative of the minor authority. The LEA nominees will be the same number as the parent governors in county schools, and that number is controlled by the number of pupils on the register of the school, although the Act lumps together all schools with 600 pupils or more.

The headteacher may decide whether or not to be a governor but is always entitled to attend normal governors' meetings. With co-options, and elected teachers, this is now the total number and categories of governors for all county schools. These are additional categories of governors for special schools (see page 80).

For voluntary schools, foundation governors are also appointed, but only aided schools may add other categories of governors, and increase the number appointed in the various categories.

Instrument of Government

For each school, the composition of the governing body is set out in the 'instrument of government'. Every governor should receive a copy on appointment, and a copy should be available at each school for people to consult. The new arrangements are set out in tabular form in Appendix 1 (page 78).

3
What Do
Governors Do?

Although governors' tasks may be described in broad general terms, legal responsibilities have recently increased, and you need to know what is expected of you as a school governor.

Governors are ordinary people. They are not expected to have detailed knowledge of modern educational practice, local authority organisation, educational finance, staff management, child care, career opportunities or building regulations – although any of these would be useful, and some knowledge is essential and can be quickly gained. What they are expected to do is to bring common sense to their task, and to satisfy themselves that the school, the local authority and the local community are serving the best interests of the pupils at the school.

The 1944 Education Act

The 1944 Education Act gave governors 'general direction of the conduct and curriculum of the school', which the headteacher manages on a day-to-day basis. The headteacher's report to the governors each term should inform them how the 'general direction' has been carried out, seek their views on the existing situation, and on any changes proposed.

Local education authorities have duties in law, and may have other policies for schools. The governors are expected to see that these duties and policies are carried out. For example, LEAs must 'so far as their powers extend . . . contribute to the spiritual, moral, mental and physical development of the community by securing that efficient education . . . shall be available to meet the needs of the population of their area'.

Articles of government

The things which governors must do, may do, and may not do are given in the 'articles of government'. The articles, together with the instrument, which establishes the board of governors and lists its composition and the rules under which it works, are legal documents, and every governor should received a copy on appointment. Their provisions cannot be ignored or altered. As the information they contain is the law of the land, the wording may be dry and legalistic, so many LEAs provide a handbook or explanatory leaflet to explain governors' powers and duties.

OVERSIGHT

Governors have to be sure that the school is being run properly, and that the children are being properly educated, so your responsibily covers:

- the curriculum – what is taught
- the 'hidden' curriculum – attitudes
- resources, such as books and materials
- discipline
- premises – buildings, playgrounds, fields
- finance
- special educational needs
- health and safety
- relations with parents
- relations with the local community
- school furnishings
- plans for change and development
- staff, and their appointment

Staff includes not only teachers. You must also consider:

- school office staff
- care assistants
- lunch-time supervisors
- caretakers and cleaners
- librarians
- laboratory and workshop technicians

Others who work at or for the school may not be employees of the LEA. For example, groundsmen may be employees of the parks and gardens department, or of an outside firm. But you may need to consider:

- kitchen staff
- crossing patrol wardens
- groundsmen

Governors should be concerned about all who work in and for the school, and may have to take up matters with other agencies if there are problems.

FINANCE

Governors have some financial responsibilites. They usually 'receive' the audited accounts of the school's private fund, and may ask questions on how the money is raised, and how it is spent. You must be informed about all the money the LEA spends on your school – on salaries, insurance, 'capitation', repairs, cleaning, caretaking and so on – and you have a duty to report on this to the parents.

SEX EDUCATION
Governors now have a special responsibility for sex education. You must decide whether sex education is to be provided in the school, and if so, you have to approve the broad content of the sex education programme.

SCHOOL RECORDS
School records on pupils are sometimes a cause of concern to parents. You should find out what records are kept, how confidential these are, and who has access to them. Do the records follow pupils to other schools? Are they used as a basis for writing references for school-leavers? Are parents able to see, and amend if necessary, records on their children?

OTHER DUTIES
Your responsibility for the conduct of the school does not end with approving the list of school rules. Governors may be called upon to decide about pupils who have been suspended from school, and you may also have to consider matters of teacher discipline.

Some of the responsibilites placed upon you will occur only occasionally: governors do not appoint new headteachers every year, or consider plans for new buildings very frequently. Some of your tasks may appear to be merely formal, although all offer scope for asking questions. In some areas, governors are given other duties, such as deciding on dates for occasional holidays, granting leave of absence to teachers, or considering the arrangements for the letting of premises. You have a duty to see that parents are informed about various aspects of the school, and once a year must prepare an annual report for parents, and follow this with an annual meeting for parents.

In voluntary schools, particularly aided schools, governors have more responsibilites, which may include choosing a teacher to be responsible for religious education, adminstering trust funds, raising money to pay for the school, and arranging the parent governor elections.

Governors are certainly not 'rubber stamps' for either the LEA or the headteacher. If you agree with the policies and proposals there may be no need to vote on them, but you should always make sure that you understand the proposals, and make your position clear if you do not agree with them.

The LEA may consult governors on a wide range of topics before introducing a new policy, and governors are entitled to make their views known to the LEA.

4
Becoming a Governor

Under the new arrangements which came into force in September 1988, there are fewer channels to becoming a governor, but there are more opportunities, especially for parents.

Being a governor should not be a reward for past political services, a circumstance for self-congratulation, or seen as a chance to air one's views on a Speech Day platform. It is a voluntary task undertaken to serve a school and the community, an opportunity to help young people to benefit fully from their education, so that in the future they, too, may wish to make their contribution to the community.

In the past many school governing bodies comprised only elected councillors and people nominated by the LEA. Membership of a local political party was one of the easiest ways to obtain nomination. With the reduction in LEA places, only the more active political party members are likely to be nominated.

Parents as governors

Increased places for elected parents offer a chance to those with children at the school. Parent governors will be able to serve for the full term of four years, and not be required to resign if they no longer have a child at the school. This could leave the current parents without full representation, so it seems wise to suggest that parents ought to resign if their child leaves the school.

In some areas, and schools, too few parents have offered

themselves for election, and many have not bothered to vote. If the school does all it can to encourage parents and to stimulate their interest, and the governors publicise the election, more people may be willing to stand for election and use their vote.

If too few parents stand for election, the governors can appoint one or more parents to fill the vacancies. Those appointed should be parents of pupils at the school, if possible, and if not, the parents of children of school age. Those so appointed must not be:

- elected members of the LEA
- employees of the LEA or any aided school maintained by the LEA
- co-opted members of any education committee of the LEA

Elections

Overall decisions about the election of parent governors are taken by the LEA (the governors, in-aided schools) but the organisation of the election may be left to the school. Any contested election must be by secret ballot.

This is the sort of procedure which could help to make the election fair, and an event of some consequence:

1 All parents with children at a school should be eligible to nominate candidates, to stand for election, and to vote. Both parents should have a vote.

2 Parents should be informed about the function of the board and their representatives.

3 Parents may not know each other, or the candidates proposed. It is desirable for each school to hold a meeting at which candidates can be proposed, and where each candidate can say something about themselves and their aspirations for the school. The meetings, however, should not all be arranged for the same day, since some parents have children in more than one school. Not all parents will be willing or able to attend this meeting, so it ought not to be the occasion on which a vote is taken. To encourage parents to attend, the meeting could be combined with some other school event, making it attractive to as many parents as possible.

4 The right to vote should not be restricted to those able to attend a meeting. After the meeting, voting papers, together with a note about each of the candidates, should be sent home to every parent, notifying them of the date for the return of the papers. If all schools' elections are in the same week, the LEA could publicise this date in the local press as a reminder. Some schools

may wish to have a voting box in school, so that parents can come in on election day to see the school and record their vote. However, other means of returning voting papers should also be acceptable.

5 The election of the parents' representatives should not be a function of the parent teacher association (PTA). Even in those schools which have a PTA (and most do not), and even where all parents are nominally members of the PTA, there will be some who do not wish to have anything to do with it. Also, PTAs, at least nominally, contain teachers, and they should not be involved in the election of the parents' representatives. At the same time, the PTA could give publicity to the election and encourage parents to vote.

6 The objection to teachers being involved in the election of the parents' representatives applies equally strongly to the headteacher and other governors, who should not even suggest possible candidates, much less nominate parents.

7 After the election, all parents should be informed in writing of the names, addresses and telephone numbers (if any) of their representatives. This information should appear on any information sent to new parents. If there is a parents' room, or noticeboard accessible to parents, the information should also appear there, perhaps accompanied by a photograph.

8 If the parent representative resigns during the period of office, another election should be held. It is not sufficient to take the 'highest loser' from the last election, or to permit only those nominated on the last occasion to stand again. All parents should be contacted as before.

One change affecting parents as a result of the 1980 Education Act is that their election makes them governors – they do not have to be confirmed by the LEA. So they may no longer be fully protected by legal support from the LEA, although the government has said that they should be equally covered by insurance. Parent governors are as entitled as any other governors to sit on sub-committees, be elected to the chair, and take a full part in the work of the governors. They cannot now be dismissed by the LEA. Indeed, there is nothing in law to show how parent governors could be removed during their period of office, although there are regulations which apply to all governors which disqualify them if they are, or become, bankrupt, or are sentenced to three or more months' imprisonment, whether or not the sentence is suspended. In those cases, governors must resign.

Other appointed and elected governors

Membership of a political party probably still offers a good chance of being appointed as a LEA governor. It is usual to find that the party with the largest majority has the most places to offer, but some are usually available to opposition party members, and sometimes the share-out is on a basis of party majority in the ward where the school is situated. You could write directly to the chairman of the education committee offering your services, especially if you have previous experience of being a governor. Your chances may be greater if you are willing to serve on a school body in a less popular area, or on a special school body.

If you are a member of one of the voluntary organisations for the disabled, your society could suggest your name for the appropriate type of special school.

Membership of a parochial church council or other church body may offer an opportunity to serve as a foundation governor of an aided or controlled school. If you are a member of a town or parish council, a minor authority, which does not itself provide an education service, you may be able to gain appointment to represent that authority on a local primary school. In the past LEAs have sometimes appointed such people to secondary-school boards, although they are under no obligation to do so, and the reduction in the number of LEA nominees may mean that they will be reluctant to do so in future.

TEACHER GOVERNORS
If you are a teacher, you are entitled to stand for election as a teacher governor of your own school.

GOVERNORS FROM INDUSTRY
If you are seeking to become a governor as a member of the local business community, you must remember that these governors will be co-opted by other members of the governing body. There may be an opportunity for your name to be included on a list of potential governors prepared by the local chamber of trade or commerce. But in many schools it is likely that nominations will be available without recourse to an official list, and it may be better to consider a direct approach. A letter to the chairman of the governors of a school with which you, or your firm, already has some connection, may be more successful. The connection may be that you have a child at the school, that your firm regularly takes pupils on work experience schemes, or employs ex-pupils, contributes to careers conventions, is a large local employer, or assists the school in some way.

Governors in this category can be of considerable help to a school. Those with experience of managing companies may have particular skills to offer. The interviewing of staff, the management of finance, a knowledge of what industry and commerce need from schools, are all useful for governors. There may be ways in which your business can help the school, with talks, visits, loans and gifts.

5
Getting Started

If you have decided, now that you know a little more about the task, to become a governor, and have been appointed or elected, there are a few practical matters to sort out.

Visiting the school

You should try to arrange a visit to the school as soon as possible, and certainly before the first meeting. Telephone the school, introduce yourself to the headteacher, and ask when a visit will be convenient. On this first occasion, the headteacher may wish to talk with you and show you round.

Remember that being a governor gives you no power at all as an individual. Any visit you make to the school, especially the first, should be by invitation. The headteacher may then invite you to 'drop in any time' thereafter, but that is a personal courtesy. Similarly, if you wish to sit in on a staff meeting or lesson, do not regard it as your right to do so. The school is the teacher's workplace, teachers have negotiated their working conditions, and are protected by their professional associations.

The governing body as a whole may make a decision about visiting, though even then they would be wise to discuss the matter with the staff first. It is common practice in some areas to appoint two governors each term to be visiting governors. Visits will be arranged at times convenient for the school and the governors. Visiting governors will prepare a report on their visit for the next meeting, and it is wise and helpful to discuss what the governors have seen during their visit, with the headteacher, before preparing the report.

Even if you know the school well, it is sensible to arrange any visit in advance, or you may find half the school on a field trip, and the other half hard at work on exams. As a new governor, you will want to know something about the school, its aspirations and problems.

Visiting the school premises includes looking at the following:

- classrooms
- halls
- gymnasium/sports hall
- dining room/kitchen
- library
- cloakrooms and toilet areas
- special rooms for art/craft/home economics, and workshops
- storage space
- playgrounds
- playing fields
- special facilities – swimming baths/parents' room/staff work-room/teaching garden/animal houses/private study areas/sixth-form common room

Try also to meet teachers and other staff, and to see children and their work.

Although you may know the school well, as a parent, or even as an ex-pupil, there will be much that you do not know about it. The headteacher is unlikely to discuss serious worries with you at this stage, except in so far as they relate to problems with the buildings or lack of resources. Such matters as poor exam results, problem teachers, difficulties with discipline or the poor esteem in which the school is held are unlikely to be aired at the first meeting. The sensible governor will not raise such matters on a first visit. For headteachers to share such worries with their governors, they have to be sure they can trust them.

Time off

If you are a working governor you may have to take time off from work in order to visit the school, and perhaps to attend meetings. The Employment Protection (Consolidation) Act 1978, and the Employment Act 1982, require employers to permit employees who hold certain public positions (which include school governorships) reasonable time off to perform their duties. 'Reasonable' is not defined, but half-a-dozen occasions a year is not likely to be considered unreasonable. Of course, if you also have time off for other public duties, as a councillor or magistrate, or for trade union activities, you cannot expect an increase in time off for being a school governor. And although some employers do pay their workers for such time off, they are not required to do so. Tribunals exist to sort out any appeals if requests for time off are refused. Let your employer know in good time if you need to take time off.

The 1986 (No 2) Education Act permits LEAs to draw up schemes to pay travelling and subsistence allowances for governors, but not loss of earnings. Only one LEA is known to have considered this, and governors may wish to press their LEA to make suitable arrangements to pay these allowances.

Information

A guide like this can only give a certain amount of information and guidance.

It cannot deal with local issues, which can sometimes be more important to local governors than some of the topics covered here. A handbook provided by the LEA may be more helpful, but is likely to deal with local policies and problems from an official point of view. It may tell you how the system works, but not how to work the system.

Training

If there is a local training scheme, try to get a place on it. Many training courses are over-subscribed for months in advance, but keep trying. The 1986 Act requires every LEA to supply every governor not just with a copy of the 'instruments and articles', but 'such other information as they (the LEA) consider appropriate in connection with the discharge of his functions as a governor' and 'that there be made available to every such governor, free of charge, such training as they (the LEA) consider necessary . . .'

While some LEAs have an enviable record for training governors, others have little or no experience of such training. Find out what your LEA offers. If it is inadequate, press for more. One of the great advantages of attending a course is that you meet governors of other schools, and other types of school. Some may be more experienced, and their experiences will be different. They may have the solutions to problems which concern you, or have found out the answers to questions which are puzzling you, and which books cannot answer.

If your LEA course is non-existent, inadequate or full, do not give up. As well as asking for more to be provided, see what other organisations are doing for governors. LEAs are not always aware that some of their own further education colleges are running governors' courses. In the past, many courses have been organised by voluntary groups, such as the Workers Educational Association, the political parties and churches, the Co-operative movement, the Campaign for the Advancement of State Education, the National Confederation of Parent-Teacher Associations, and the National Association of Governors and Managers.

Training provided by voluntary bodies is unlikely to be free, but charges should be modest, and all training is worthwhile. However, be wary of the 'commercial' training operations now being mounted by some private organisations, who may offer a 'package' on topics such as financial management, with fees running into hundreds of pounds.

Governors from industry and commerce will be as much in need of training as others, and schemes of training for governors from the business community are already in existence. Some training for governors from the business community is being prepared by 'Industry Matters'. (Details about organisations offering training appear on page 77.)

SELF-HELP
There are self- or group-training packages available. Some governing

bodies and parents' groups have undertaken their own training, using such packages or the Open University course. Although this is now becoming out of date, it does contain much useful material, and copies have been given to LEAs. If your governing body decides on a self-training scheme, your LEA might be able to lend you an Open University pack. With the help of the headteacher and clerk, group training of this kind is not difficult, although you lose the exchange of ideas and experience with other governors which a course gives.

6
Who Makes the Decisions?

When you become a governor, you will be working with other groups to make decisions. This chapter looks at those groups, what their powers and functions are, and how you as a governor will relate to them.

The local education authority (LEA)

The LEA is responsible for providing and maintaining all state schools in its area. The LEA is the council, and it usually works through an education committee. This consists of elected councillors, although there may also be co-opted people from the churches, higher education and the local business community. There may also be representatives of teachers and parents.

Although the LEA is bound by certain national standards, such as the age for compulsory education, and how much can be spent on school buildings, it can also make decisions which others must follow, such as:

- whether schools are primary or secondary
- whether schools are mixed or single-sex
- whether schools are comprehensive or selective
- the age of transfer from primary to secondary education
- the way in which parents can choose schools

With other governors

It is important to know your fellow governors and whom they represent. While 'cliques' on governing bodies are to be deplored, you may, nevertheless, find it helpful to work with one or two other governors from time to time, in certain aspects of your work. Parent governors, in particular, may find it helpful to work together. This may be done by meeting together before the termly meeting to go through the agenda, the headteacher's report and other papers. You may need further information or help in understanding some of the issues – even the words, since education is full of jargon. You may wish to take a joint approach to some topics, and decide who shall put forward which points.

On some issues, parent and teacher governors may wish to work together. Teachers are sometimes diffident about raising topics in the headteacher's presence, and parents may be able to ask questions without disclosing the teachers' concern.

LEA governors may meet together, perhaps with governors from other schools, for a termly briefing, and to decide their attitude to items which affect many schools. Foundation governors may be similarly briefed. Teacher governors meet in their staff rooms, but parent and co-opted governors may need to make special arrangements to meet, if they feel a need to do so.

These suggestions are not intended to give the impression that everyone meets in their groups before every meeting, to decide what they will do at the meeting. Governors' meetings do not consist of a series of armed camps, each totally opposing the views of all the others. No one should vote on an issue, or decide, finally, their point of view, until they have listened to the debate, and heard the views of others. Governors do, generally, work amicably together. On many issues it is not necessary to take a vote, since all are in agreement.

With parents

Governors have a particular duty towards parents of their school's pupils. You must ensure that parents are informed about the school. You have to approve the school booklet, prepare an annual report for parents, and hold an annual meeting for them. While parent governors are likely to be best known to other parents, and therefore more likely to be approached for information or help, parents may turn to any governor.

Some LEAs urge governors to develop relationships with the parent body. Here are some suggestions, already in use by parent governors, which could help all governors to become known to the parents:

- All parents should be told the name, address and telephone number of the school's governors. Being a governor is a public office, and the public must be able to contact the office holders.
- Governors could wear name badges at all meetings they attend in school when parents are present. As well as plays and concerts, schools may like to invite governors to every function when parents are present, and invite them to sports events and field-trips, too.
- If there is a parents' noticeboard, details of governors, with photographs, could be given there.
- A note about new governors could appear in a local community or parish newsletter.
- Some parent governors send a letter to parents each term, or this could be included in a school newsletter.

With the local community

Some, at least, of the governors should be members of the local community, able to pass on to it information about the school, and to the school information about the views of the community. You may find yourself having to correct mistaken or out-of-date views about the school, or tell the school that some of its activities are causing concern to its neighbours: for example, local dogs may be spoiling playing fields; teachers' car parking may be causing problems for residents.

Good relations with the local community can help the school in many ways. In some areas, local people form a 'School Watch', to be on the look-out for trespassers or vandalism, especially if there is no resident caretaker. A community school, with facilities which are used by local people – clinic, library, sports facilities and so on – has excellent opportunities to develop good relations with its neighbours. You should at least be aware of such possibilities, and do your best to develop links with the community.

With ethnic minorities

If your school is in an area where there are pupils from ethnic minority homes, you may have to consider whether your annual report – and the school booklet and other information for parents – should be produced in languages other than English. If you are a member of such a community, you may be able to help the school and the community in a number of ways:

- by helping to develop strong links between the school and your community
- by offering to translate papers, or suggesting someone who could help in this way
- by encouraging members of your community to be involved with the school as governors, or in the parents' association, or in other ways
- by helping the school and other governors to know and understand the aspirations and views of your community as affected by the school

If your school has no representatives of ethnic-minority communities on its governors, you can try to remedy this when you are considering co-options. If no one is willing to be co-opted, try inviting (through the chairman) an observer or two, to each meeting.

If your school has no pupils from ethnic minority homes, you could find out what steps the school takes to make pupils aware of the multi-cultural society into which they will move on leaving school.

With the churches

Especially in a voluntary school, you will need to develop a relationship with the church authorities and the local parish. Foundation governors will provide an official link, but other governors also need to be aware of the special relationship. In aided schools this is even more vital, since part of the money for the school comes from the foundation.

With others

You may be surprised to learn that the chief officer of police is entitled to express a view on the curriculum of the school. Others who use the school premises, such as youth groups, adult classes and local businesses, may all have views about the school which you should consider. Schools have many relationships which extend beyond the school, and you need to be aware of the links which exist with services and agencies in the community, which serve the needs of your pupils, or are in some way affected by decisions which you make.

Working together

Headteachers usually set the 'style' of the school, and may work in quite different ways. You have to find out where you fit in and relate to the headteacher and staff, as well as the other governors. How formal or informal is the relationship? How well do the governors work together? To be effective, you must be clear about what needs to be done, what is possible and how to set about it. Developing contacts in and outside the school is useful. Keeping up to date with changes in education in the LEA is helpful. Being willing to give time in invaluable. Most schools welcome extra pairs of hands, and extra resources. An extra adult helper on school outings, waste materials in quantity, help with school clubs and societies, visits to factories, help with money-raising activities and school social occasions will all be appreciated, and many of these will bring governors into closer contact with parents, staff and pupils.

When you are seen to be a person who has the welfare of the school at heart, who is willing to work for it and take trouble for it, and when a sense of trust has developed between school and governor, you are much more likely to be taken into the confidence of the headteacher and staff if there are problems.

Assessing

Trust is a two-way thing, and has to be earned, but it does not mean a blind acceptance of everything you are told; you need to check, as well. When you visit the school, keep your eyes open. You may spot potential hazards, dubious cleaning, tired displays which the familiar eyes of the teachers have missed. If you hear of problems which are concerning the local community, find out the basis of them. Are they true? Have steps been taken to improve matters? Don't just adopt the attitude 'my school, right or wrong'. Try not to be so close to the school that you are blind to defects. It may sometimes be difficult to maintain a balance between total support for the school and being critical of everything it does, but, as a governor, you must try.

Helping

Parents and staff may seek your help. Problems may be resolved without always having to discuss them at a governors' meeting, but be sure that the chairman is aware if there are problems.

As a governor, your aim is not to be popular, but to serve the school, its staff, pupils and community. If you can do that effectively, you will have done all that is required of you. Anything else is a bonus.

8
The Board Meeting

What happens at meetings? Who is in charge? What is the business of the meeting? Will you have a chance to speak? In this chapter, we look at these and other questions.

Time and place

Governors' meetings must be held at least once in each term. Dates and times are usually arranged at least a term in advance. Every effort should be made to attend, and to stay for the whole meeting. If this is not possible, send a written apology, in advance, to the clerk or chairman. People who miss all the meetings in a year cease to be governors.

Meetings may be held in school time, which means you can see the school in action. An evening meeting may mean more people can attend, and it can go on longer, although that is not always an advantage. A mixture of day and evening meetings may help most people to attend.

Meetings are usually held in the school, but if it is very small, they may be held at another suitable place.

Style of meetings

Meetings may be very informal, especially if governors know each other well. You may sit in the staff room, and only the headteacher, clerk and chairman have a table for their papers. Or the meeting may be more formal, in the school hall or library, with all governors sitting round a table. The style and tone of the meeting will be set not only by the meeting place, but also by

the chairman. Meetings should not be so informal that the business is lost in chatter, nor so formal that governors hesitate to speak up, or ask questions. Asking questions, to satisfy yourself that all is well, is one of the main ways in which governors work. What to ask questions about, how to ask them, and how to interpret the answers are skills which have to be acquired, and which are difficult to teach. Sometimes, you may have to appear a little naive in asking a question so that you can get an answer that everyone can understand. Sometimes, a question may be asked in a way which conceals its true purpose. Sometimes, too, you need to know what questions not to ask, especially on appointments (see chapter 10).

The Chairman

This may be a man or a woman, and may be called 'chair' or 'chairperson'. But since Acts of Parliament refer to 'chairman' that is the term used here. The chairman is elected by the other governors, and any governor may be chairman except a person employed at the school (some LEAs bar anyone employed by the LEA or the council). As well as chairing meetings, the chairman is given authority to act for the governors between meetings.

The chairman may need to be available to visit the school between meetings, to deal with routine matters or sudden emergencies. You will probably want to contact the chairman if you have a serious concern about the school which you cannot discuss with the headteacher, or which the headteacher thinks is not a problem, or not serious.

At the meeting, the chairman runs the proceedings. He or she may call on other governors for a point of view if they have not contributed to a discussion, so be prepared. Usually, the chairman will judge when a debate has covered all angles, and will then call for a vote. Voting may not be needed, because decisions are often reached by general agreement. 'Do you accept the report?': nods all round. Voting is by show of hands, counted by the clerk. If there is a tie, the chairman has a second vote, and this is usually exercised in favour of the present situation, as in most committee meetings, rather than for a change.

The clerk or correspondent

A representative of the chief education officer is entitled to attend all governors' meetings, and in many LEAs will act as clerk. In church schools, the clerk may be called the correspondent. Or the clerk may be the school secretary, or one of the governors, or an outside person. Unless the clerk is a governor, he or she has no vote. If you do not have an LEA officer as clerk, and no officer attends the meeting, you could ask for one to be present, especially if you are dealing with something which is not straight-forward or routine.

The clerk's main functions are:
- to take minutes, unless someone else does this
- to report back on what has happened to your resolutions
- to arrange the agenda with the chairman
- to advise you on legal aspects of your work, and LEA policy
- to advise you on correct procedure
- to help you to frame resolutions
- to ensure that the agenda, reports and minutes are sent to governors
- to inform you of arrangements for training, and perhaps to organise it.

If you, as a governor, are asked to act as clerk, find out what is involved. Some lay clerks have to produce and post the papers to governors, and may not be repaid the cost of doing so for several months.

If the clerk is absent, you can appoint another person for the meeting, and if the clerk is unsatisfactory, you can ask the LEA to appoint someone else. The LEA cannot change your clerk without consulting you.

Clerks who are LEA officers can often help, through their contacts in the department, to speed responses to your concerns. In aided schools, the correspondent may need to have knowledge of contract and employment laws.

The agenda

About a week before the meeting, you should receive the agenda, which gives details of the meeting, and a list of the business. The headteacher's report and other papers should be included with the agenda. Do make time to go through the papers, marking any points about which you have a question, or anything which is not there which you want to ask for. You can ask for an item to be put on to the agenda by contacting the chairman or clerk. To be sure of inclusion, you should ask before the agenda is prepared, but the chairman may be willing to add the item at the end of the agenda if you ask before the meeting. If you wish to put forward a proposal for debate and decision by the whole board, it may be helpful to word it in advance, and decide who will propose and who will second the proposal. From time to time, you may wish to arrange a meeting with the headteacher, to indicate points you intend to raise. so that answers are available at the meeting. It is frustrating to ask a question, and be told that the answer will be given at the next meeting, which may be months away. Sometimes it may be better not to show your hand before the meeting.

For an ordinary meeting, the agenda will usually contain these items:
- apologies for absence
- confirmation of the minutes of the previous meeting
- matters arising from those minutes
- urgent business since the last meeting – or 'chairman's action'
- headteacher's report
- sub-committee reports
- reports from the LEA
- any other reports
- finance
- confidential items

- any other urgent business
- notices
- date of next meeting

If the agenda is not completed, the governors can agree to adjourn to another date to finish it. It is not sufficient to pass uncompleted items to the chairman, or to the next meeting.

If you are faced with an enormous agenda, with many reports, you may be tempted to skip reading them beforehand, and hope to pick up the information as the meeting proceeds. The other governors may accept a report without discussion, and you may lose the chance to ask a vital question, if you have not done your homework.

MINUTES

Minutes are a record of who was present, what was done and what was decided. They are not a complete record of all discussion points. You will be asked to agree that the minutes are accurate. If they are not, say so. The chairman will sign them, and then a copy will be kept in the school, which may be consulted by school staff, parents of registered pupils, and the pupils themselves. Any confidential matters are excluded from this copy.

If you want to know whether an item is confidential, ask at the end of the discussion on it. Some governors decide at the end of the meeting what is confidential. Generally, anything about an individual teacher, pupil or pupil's family is confidential. So too may be anything on proposed changes to the school which are not yet public. Names of pupils rarely need to be given to governors, whether they are discussing those with special needs, or those who are special problems. Pupils whom the headteacher wishes to commend, or who have given some particular service, can, of course, be named and the governors may wish to add their good wishes or thanks.

MATTERS ARISING

There should be a report to you which updates anything from the previous meeting, and the result of your requests or resolutions at the last meeting. If these are missing, or inadequate, you may wish to take further action (see page 71). Alternatively you could ask the chairman, headteacher or clerk to investigate further. If you must accept the response you have received, consider whether there is any other way you could achieve the desired result.

URGENT ITEMS

This is where the chairman reports to you any urgent matters he or she has dealt with on behalf of the governors since the last meeting. This may have been a temporary closure of the school due to a boiler failure, or seeing a parent about the temporary exclusion of a pupil. Was the action appropriate, was the need urgent, or could it have waited for a regular meeting of the governors? In accepting this report, you are endorsing the action taken by the chairman in your name.

THE HEADTEACHER'S REPORT
This is usually the main item of business, and the next chapter is devoted to it.

SUB-COMMITTEE REPORTS
The governors may have set up sub-committees, on a variety of topics, such as staffing, finance, equal opportunities, or to draft the annual report. Sub-committees should report back to the full meeting. They may have some recommendations which they wish you to endorse, or some questions they wish you to discuss.

REPORTS FROM THE LEA
These may be going to all schools, or to a limited group. They may be 'for information only', or seek responses from you. If a change involving your school is planned, you will want to be sure you have all the relevant information, and time to consult parents, staff and pupils before you have to reply.

OTHER REPORTS
The governors may have asked for special reports. These may be from the headteacher and staff, or from LEA officers, or from other bodies, such as the road safety department on parking problems, or a bus company about their service to the school, or from diocesan authorities in church schools.

FINANCE
Each year, your LEA must tell you the total costs involved for your school, including all the staffing costs. It must also make available to you a sum of money which you can allocate to various items, according to LEA guidelines. Some LEAs have given governors the responsibility of spending the whole of the school's capitation allowance. This is the sum of money for books and equipment, based on an amount per pupil, and varying with the ages of pupils. You may delegate the spending of this sum to the headteacher, but if so, the allocation of it must be reported to you.

A few areas have given the governors of some schools the power to decide on the spending of large sums of money, allocated by the LEA, to meet most of the costs of running the school. This includes:

- all staff costs – salaries and wages, but not pensions. It includes 'cover' for short absences
- books, equipment of all kinds, furniture, paper and other supplies
- cleaning and minor repairs
- rent and rates

By September 1989, LEAs must draw up plans to extend schemes of this kind to all secondary schools and all primary schools with more than 200 pupils; and they may, if they wish, cover all schools. A minimum level of staffing will be included, but beyond that, governors will have discretion to spend on additional staff, or use their allocation for other purposes.

Some funds will be retained by the LEA, to pay for centrally provided services, for cover for longer absences, major building or repairs and some other costs, but all the rest of their budget will be allocated to schools. There will be rules and guidelines for spending the allocation. The governors may delegate to the headteacher, so far as their local plan permits, their powers under these local management schemes, though the proposals made by the head-teacher must be reported to them. The governors may not spend the money in a way which the headteacher considers would be inconsistent with the educational requirements of the school.

Some of the schools which already have the power to spend the sum allocated in this way have found they are able to provide more staff and equipment. LEAs have found that they need to employ more staff to assist and advise the governors who have these new powers.

Governors are also often given responsibility for receiving the audited accounts of the school's private funds. This is money raised by parents, staff and pupils to buy things which the capitation allowance does not cover, and which are not essential items which the LEA must provide.

You may also be asked to consider gifts to the school, perhaps from the parents' association. If these will need to be repaired or serviced by the LEA, you should find out whether they are willing to bear these future costs before accepting the gift. For example, a mini-bus is a wonderful gift, but who pays for petrol, licence, insurance, servicing, testing and so on?

Even if the governors set up a finance sub-committee, there will be times when the whole board must consider finance.

CONFIDENTIAL ITEMS

Governors' meetings are public meetings, and are covered by the same rules as, for example, council meetings, so press and public are entitled to attend as observers. Non-governors can be excluded during the consideration of any confidential item, so some governors divide their agenda into two parts.

Most matters can be discussed in part one, after which non-governors leave, and confidential items can be reported and discussed. These may include details about pupils with special needs, pupils who are suspended or excluded from school, concerns which might be damaging to the school if publicly reported at this stage, and, in aided schools, details of tenders and so on. These are matters which may be excluded from the minutes made available in the school.

OTHER URGENT BUSINESS

This may be something which has arisen since the agenda and reports were prepared, or on which a governor did not have previous knowledge of a problem. It is not the place for general questions, or for matters which can wait until another meeting.

NOTICES

These may include training courses or conferences for governors, or forthcoming school events.

SPECIAL ITEMS

Sometimes you will find an item on your agenda which is not there at every meeting.

Elections

At the first meeting of the year you will have to consider the election of chairman and vice-chairman. The clerk (or the previous chairman) will take the chair, and call for nominations. If this is the first meeting of the new body members may not know each other, so do take any opportunity offered to meet before the meeting. If you wish to nominate a governor as chairman, obtain that person's consent, and ask another governor to second the nomination. To avoid any problem which may arise in suggesting a second name, when one has been suggested, you can send your nomination, in writing, to the clerk before the meeting. If necessary, the clerk conducts the election, which can be by show of hands. The elected chairman then conducts the election of a vice-chairman.

Co-options

At the first meeting of a new body (every four years) you will be asked to consider co-options. You may wish to invite a former governor, or someone who has been or can be of service to the school, to join the governors. Governors must consider whether the local business community is adequately represented on the board, perhaps by a parent or LEA nominee. If not, they must use one or more of their co-optative places to bring in people who appear to be members of that community.

It is always sensible to have names ready to suggest, with the agreement of the people concerned. You may wish to suggest people who already have a connection with the school, as parents or members of businesses which contribute to the school in some way, perhaps by offering work-experience placements for pupils, or large local employers, or trade unionists. Or you may be able to choose a name from a list supplied by the local chamber of commerce, though these are less likely to be known to you.

Delegation of functions
Your articles should tell you what you can delegate to the headteacher, the chairman or a sub-committee. The governors may decide to set up a sub-committee to deal with finance, buildings, pupil discipline or some other topic. If so, there should be a report on the topic at future meetings.

Annual report to parents
Governors must report each year on what they have done during the previous year. Certain information must be given: details about governors, examination results and the finances of the school. Even if a sub-committee prepares a draft report, governors should ensure that the report is agreed by them. The report must be distributed, free of charge, to all parents and guardians and school staff, and to anyone else who is entitled to see it, such as prospective parents. You have to decide whether there is a need to produce your report in a minority language or languages, and arrange for this to be done. Because of the costs involved, it is usual for the report to be taken home by pupils.

Finance
You may find that a longer discussion on finance is arranged when you are to consider the budget.

9
The Headteacher's Report

Although the report is your main source of information, term by term, about the school, you will also need to visit and talk to others who have a full picture of your school. The report will contain facts, but there may also be questions about plans for the future which governors will be expected to discuss.

Every aspect of the school may be mentioned at some time in the report, but certain items should be included each term. While you may learn something about the school from a list of visitors, football match results and a grumble about litter, and use these as a basis for questions, they are not sufficient for you to be able to carry out your responsibility for the conduct and curriculum of the school.

The report may be formal or chatty, but it is a report to governors, not a letter to the chairman, or a few odd notes on the back of an envelope.

If the report has been circulated, there is no need for the headteacher to read it out, though the chairman can ask if there is anything which has come up since the report was prepared.

Reports for primary schools may be shorter, and have fewer items, but they should cover most of those listed below.

These items should be included:

Staff

Once a year, governors should receive a list of all staff, including non-teaching staff, and their area and level of responsibility. At each meeting, changes can be reported:

- New probationer teachers – how are they settling in?
- Resignations – have staff left on promotion?
- Internal promotions – were governors involved?
- Appointments of staff – were governors involved?
- Retirements – governors may wish to convey thanks and good wishes.

The headteacher may be concerned about staffing in the future because of:

- Problems of recruiting for some subjects or areas of work – e.g. cleaners
- new needs in the curriculum
- staff reductions to be made because of falling rolls

Staff training may be reported, in particular:

- staff attendance at courses, conferences and in-service training days
- initiatives on training in the school – this may be more appropriate under 'curriculum'
- training devised in the school and offered to other schools.

Sometimes, topics raised at staff meetings may have implications for governors. The teacher governors can be asked to comment directly on relevant items.

Other governors may wish to ask about aspects of staffing. Once a year, the headteacher should report the proposed staffing structure for the following year. Changed numbers of pupils, new initiatives on the curriculum, staff changes and government regulations may all affect the way a school is organised, and you should have a clear picture of this, and its staffing implications. Some of these may indicate a need for more office staff rather than more teachers, and governors should be clear what policy changes will mean for non-teaching as well as teaching staff.

Teachers now have to work a fixed number of hours each year, under the direction of the headteacher. The work to which they are directed may include evening meetings for parents, training days, field trips and excursions, as well as classroom teaching and administrative or pastoral duties.

Teachers now have one main grade for pay. Some allowances are available for teachers with special responsibilities, and governors should be told how many of these are available in the school and how they are allocated.

Pupils

NUMBERS

Once a year, governors should be given the number of children in each year, divided into figures for each sex, where appropriate. Changes expected during the year, as more children start school, or leave at the end of their period of compulsory schooling, should be indicated, too, since these figures may affect staffing, accommodation and resources. Factors which you will need to note include:

- changing birth rate in the catchment area
- changes in housing locally, such as demolition, new house building, changes in use, or when high-rise flats are no longer used for families with young children
- changes in the number of pupils staying at school after the age of 16.

Arrangements at the beginning and end of children's school days should also be reported to governors:

- Have new pupils been admitted to the school?
- Did they come from other schools?
- What links are there with senior schools to which pupils transfer?
- What is the destination of pupils leaving the school?
- Did they transfer to other schools, to further or higher education?
- What links are there with contributory schools, nurseries and playgroups?
- What numbers of pupils went to other educational establishments?
- How many went into employment or training schemes? How many are unemployed?

ACHIEVEMENTS

The results of public examinations have to be published and included in the governors' annual report to parents. Details should be reported to governors, perhaps in an appendix, and the headteacher could highlight particular aspects of the results in the report. You should also be informed of pupils' other achievements: academic, sporting and social (although it is not necessary to include details of all matches played by school teams in every report). If there is a school council, a report on topics discussed may be included.

FAMILY BACKGROUND

The number of pupils who receive free school meals or other grants, or who come from one-parent families, may give a guide on the social problems faced by parents and the school. If the school has children for whom English is not the language of the home, this should be reported to the governors. You will need to know what steps are being taken by the school to respond to the needs of such pupils, and to communicate with their parents. In some secondary schools, religious feasts and fasts (especially Ramadan) may have a marked effect on the life of the school.

SPECIAL NEEDS

Governors should know of the number of children in the school who have special educational needs. Some of these may have a 'statement of special educational need', drawn up jointly by teachers and specialists of many kinds, and discussed and agreed with the child's parents. The statement will include details of special help to be provided for the child. There will be others who, although not 'statemented', do have needs which the school must try to meet. You have a duty as a governor to use your best endeavours to ensure that the needs of these children are met by the school and the education service.

Many more young people who are in some way handicapped are now educated in mainstream rather than special schools, and provisions must be made for them, whether they require ramps for wheel-chair access, a room for special toiletting needs, or additional teaching help. Sometimes a unit may be attached to the school, so that a number of similarly handicapped pupils can be provided with suitable teachers and facilities, for example for deaf or blind children. A report on the work and needs of such a unit should be included regularly for governors.

PROBLEMS

Governors should receive regular reports on attendance and truancy, lateness, and behaviour problems. You should know, and have approved, the school rules, and monitor how well these are observed. The sanctions used by the school for problems of attendance and misbehaviour should also be known. You should have discussed the setting up of any special facilities – withdrawal units and similar arrangements – to deal with problems, and you need to know how well these are working, and what success they have in returning pupils to ordinary classes.

If any pupils have been suspended from school, whether or not they have been readmitted, this should be reported. Governors should be able to monitor whether any particular group in the school is causing problems, and what action is being taken to improve matters (see also page 73).

The section of the headteacher's report which deals with pupils may be the place to discuss policy on admissions, the effect of 'open access' (see page 72) and the problems arising from falling or rising numbers. But any discussion on amalgamation, closure or additional premises needs a separate agenda item.

Curriculum

Governors now have increased responsibility for the curriculum. Chapter 12 on the curriculum goes into detail about this, but the governors will have been informed about the LEA's policy, and will have helped to draw up the school's policy statement. In order to monitor how well this is working, you will need regular reports from the headteacher. You should also consider the views of staff and parents, and must take note of any views expressed by the local chief officer of police, so far as his area of responsibility is concerned.

In primary schools, as well as what is taught, and how, and with what success, there should be some information on how the school helps new pupils to settle in happily, the involvement of parents in their children's learning, how the curriculum relates to, and links up with, later stages of education, and the social education of young children.

The curriculum is not just about subjects, although the governors should be informed about progress and achievements in reading

and maths, which are regularly monitored in the school once a year, so that they can assess how well the school is achieving its objectives. They could also be told about other aspects of the curriculum, and how many children can swim, or play a musical instrument, before they move on to secondary education.

Within the curriculum area, there will be policies which apply to the whole school: such matters as homework, assessment and marking, the use of information technology, study skills, policies on equal opportunities and racial equality. You should take particular note of how these are working. Future developments which are contemplated should be discussed with the governors, together with information about preparations for any curriculum development, which will probably involve staff training, extra resources and a monitoring scheme to judge the success of new initiatives.

Premises, furniture and equipment

The headteacher's report should regularly inform you about the state of the buildings, playgrounds and fields, including boundary walls.

The headteacher should report regularly on the need for repairs and replacements of furniture and equipment, and new equipment needed. Repairs, in particular, can take up a great deal of time at governors' meetings, if allowed to do so, and many boards prefer to set up a sub-committee to work with the school staff and officers of the LEA on such matters.

Sometimes a piece of equipment required by the school may be bought from funds raised by parents. Make sure that the donors are thanked, and ensure that the LEA is willing to insure the gift, and meet its upkeep costs.

Health and safety

So far as both premises and equipment are concerned, you should be particularly aware of the health and safety of pupils and staff. Whether you are there as a visiting governor, or are simply making an ordinary visit to the school, you should note the state of the buildings and facilities, not only in the teaching and playing spaces, but in dining and cloakrooms, the staff room and school office. Not everyone has a dedication to detail of this sort, but headteachers and school staff do not always complain when their own conditions are poor, and you should be concerned about good conditions for staff as well as pupils.

Parents

From time to time, the headteacher should report on various aspects of the school's relations with parents. This may be arrangements for parents of future pupils to visit, parental involvement in the careers programme, regular forms of information sent to parents, meetings and discussions in any home–school association, the regular use of parents in school, consultations with parents on new developments or subject options, and so on. Governors may like to receive an invitation to events and meetings organised by or for parents.

Community use of premises

Increasingly schools are used, in and out of school hours, by other members of the community. The activities may be organised by the school: after-hours clubs and sports, with parents helping. Or there may be lettings of the school hall and other facilities, for which the governors may have been given some responsibility. The school may have adult education classes or a youth club using its premises in the evenings. You should be informed about such arrangements, and any problems which arise.

Visitors

The headteacher's report may contain a list of visitors to the school, ranging from Her Majesty's Inspectors (HMIs) to the supervisor of caretakers or school meals superintendent.

Visits and excursions

You should be told of out-of-school visits. Some LEAs require governors to approve the arrangements for overnight and overseas visits arranged by the school, whether these are solely recreational or part of the education programme, and whether they are in holiday or school time. You should be clear about the arrangements for all out-of-school visits.

- Are parents fully informed, and their consent obtained? For all-day, overnight and overseas visits, this should be in writing.
- Is there a charge to parents?
- Are children unable to go if parents are unwilling or unable to pay?
- Are there arrangements for meeting the cost of pupils whose parents are unable to pay all or part of the charge?

- What supervision arrangements have been made? Are they satisfactory?
- Are parents (or governors) invited to accompany such visits? How many do?
- What arrangements are made for the children who remain in school during a visit?

Special topics

From time to time, the headteacher may include in the report details of some special initiative, information requested by governors, or details of national or local developments. Links with other schools or with the local community, a project involving the whole school, or a report prepared by a head of house, year or subject, may offer you another view of the school. There is no need for the headteacher to write every word of the report, and some headteachers regularly call on another member of staff to report on some aspect of the school, such as building repairs needed, heating problems, or a section of the school (perhaps the nursery or infants, in a school which covers the whole of the primary age-range). Such reports can be added as appendices to the main report, as can details of exam results and staff responsibilities.

Using the report

I have indicated some of the aspects of the school on which you should expect to receive regular or occasional reports. Governors sometimes complain that they are not told much about the curriculum of the school, or about conduct, but only about repairs needed, visitors to the school, fund-raising and outings. Even with these few topics, questions can reveal much more, and you can always ask for the form and content of the report to be changed. Some headteachers, especially those new to the post, may never have attended a governors' meeting before, and may be uncertain what governors want to know. Some headteachers may give you a lot of statistics which are difficult to assess. Ask for a general picture, with the detailed statistics as an appendix.

You could use some items in the report to gain a more detailed picture by asking questions about them:
- Was the HMI's visit a routine one, or will a report be made to the governors?

- Was it connected with a particular aspect of the school, and what did the HMI have to say about the visit?
- If a local inspector or advisor visited, was this in connection with an aspect of the curriculum?
- Has there been a caretaking problem that needed the attention of the supervisor?
- Did the parent who came into school to talk about their job take part in a regular series of talks as part of the careers programme, or as a contribution to study of some aspect of the curriculum?
- Did the nurse/doctor/dentist/health visitor note any particular problems?
- Were the outings part of an ongoing study of some area of the curriculum?
- How much preparatory work was involved, for staff and pupils?
- What follow-up work has there been?
- Is there to be a display about the visit – photos, pictures, written work, etc – which the governors could see?

If governors indicate what they want from the report, give evidence of having read it, ask questions, and answer – or at least discuss – any questions that the head has posed for them in the report, they are more likely to receive interesting and informative reports in the future. You will also learn much that you need to know to carry out your tasks properly.

10
Special meetings

You may be called to a special meeting to deal with something which is urgent, or needs more time for consideration. At these meetings, as at staff appointment meetings, you may only consider items on the agenda, not any other matters.

Appointments

Governors now have a responsibility in the appointment of senior staff, and are often involved in the appointment of other staff. In the future, when local management schemes operate, this responsibility could be increased.

You may have to arrange for the post to be advertised, then consider all the applications, and draw up a short-list of candidates to be interviewed. Arrangements differ in different areas: if in doubt, consult your articles. Do not let anyone try to bend the rules – for example, by suggesting that you do not need to undertake some part of the process. Appointing staff, especially senior staff, or any who will be in contact with the public outside the school, is one of the most important tasks governors undertake.

HEADTEACHER
The appointment of a new headteacher can affect the lives of generations of pupils and the careers of school staff, and can have a profound effect on many aspects of life in the neighbourhood, perhaps for many years. For an appointment of this importance, the governing body should insist on having sufficient time to do the job properly. Governors, who represent the whole community served by the school, should be fully involved.

Your first task should be to consider the kind of person you will be looking for to fill the post. Sometimes, the LEA does the shortlisting. If governors are empowered to shortlist, you can choose applicants most suited to your school; if the LEA shortlists, you will have to choose among people who, while acceptable to the LEA, may not be entirely suitable for your school.

If you are not impressed by any of the candidates, you can ask for the post to be re-advertised. Because of school closures and reductions in size, many LEAs have to redeploy existing teachers, and you may have to consider these first. Sometimes, because of falling rolls, only teachers already employed at the school can be considered for posts.

INTERVIEWING
If you have to choose which governors will act on behalf of the board to interview candidates, it is sensible to consider having both people who are experienced governors or experienced interviewers, and others who need to gain experience.

The professional experience and competence, both teaching and administrative, of the candidates will be mainly covered by the officers who assist the selectors, and by the headteacher, if the post is not the headship. After you are satisfied about these, your main concern will be the personality of the candidates, which may not be easy to determine in a short period. Governors can help to put candidates at their ease by asking questions in a friendly manner. Here are some suggested questions:

- Can you tell us about something you have done in your present post which has been successful?
- Has your hobby or interest in . . . been of assistance to you in teaching?
- How helpful was the course you attended on . . .?

You may wish to ask about any obvious changes in the career direction of candidates:

- You came into teaching from industry. Have you found your previous job has helped you in teaching?
- I see you had a period out of teaching. Can you tell us something about the job you did then?

There are some questions which you may *not* ask:

- about a candidate's political or religious opinions or membership
- about a candidate's union or professional association affiliations
- about how a candidate would organise their private life if appointed. It may be appropriate to ask if they intend to move into the area if appointed, or if their present address would involve long journeys to the school

• about a candidate's sexual orientation

You may like to make short notes about each candidate seen, so that you can recall them clearly in the discussion which will follow the interview. Do not try to award each candidate a mark out of 10 for speech, appearance, experience and so on, and then add up each person's marks: this is not a suitable way to assess who will best fit the post.

After the interview you may be able to eliminate some of the candidates, and then consider the remainder. There will probably be no perfect candidate, and you will then have to consider experience versus warmth of personality, further training versus enthusiasm, and so on. References will be given, and if the candidates are already employed by your LEA, there may be a confidential report. Present practice is towards more open references, seen by the candidates, so you may have to 'read between the lines'.

If your LEA officer suggests that a candidate is not suitable, without explanation, try to find out the reason for this view. You should at least insist that the chairman is told the reason. There may be a good reason for not giving the information to all the governors. For example, if the candidate is an internal applicant, governors' future relations with that person may be affected adversely. Or the information may reflect badly on another person or institution. If the chairman has been informed and is satisfied with the reasons given, governors may be willing to accept that the reasons are sound, but better not publicised. This is likely to be a very rare event. Governors may still insist on being told the reason, but should be aware of and willing to accept any consequences.

At the end of the discussions, you should be able to recommend one candidate for appointment, or ask for the post to be re-advertised. Any information you gain about candidates is, of course, confidential.

WITHDRAWAL

Any governor who is, or whose relative is, a candidate for a post at the school, should not take part at any stage in the arrangements for filling the post. The headteacher should not be at all involved in steps to find a successor. If the deputy headteacher is a candidate, he or she should not take part, of course, nor should any staff governor who may be a candidate for the deputy headship, if the present incumbent should be appointed to the headship.

Governors must declare an interest, and withdraw from any discussions on matters in which they have a pecuniary interest, such as a contract. Nor may governors take part in discussion about promotion, transfer or retirement of a member of staff, if they or a relative living with them could be a candidate for the post. A governor cannot take part in reaching a decision if disciplinary action is being considered against that governor, or against a pupil or school employee, over a matter in which the governor is involved other than as a governor (for example, as a parent or teacher). They may be present to speak on such matters, to hear allegations or give relevant evidence, but should not take part in decisions.

Staff discipline

You may sometimes be required to act in a quasi-judicial way, if a staff member is the subject of complaint or dispute. The event is rare, and you should be fully briefed beforehand by your LEA officer. The LEA will have a code of conduct and a grievance procedure, drawn up in conjunction with local representatives of teachers' associations. If a teacher is accused of a disciplinary offence, or is in dispute with the headteacher or

another teacher, they may be entitled to appear before the governors, accompanied by a 'friend' who will usually be an officer of the teacher's professional association or union.

Having heard all the evidence, you may be called upon for a decision. You may wish to recommend:

- that the complaint is ill-founded
- that no further action should be taken
- that the teacher should be warned about future conduct
- that the teacher should be moved elsewhere
- that the teacher should undergo a further period of training
- that the teacher should be dismissed

Pupil discipline

More frequently, you may have to consider pupil discipline. You need to be clear about the situation when a school refuses to continue to admit a pupil. Schools stand 'in the place of the parent' (in loco parentis), and this responsibility can extend beyond the school walls and the school day. If a pupil behaves badly, the school may wish to hand back the responsibility to the parents, who still have a duty to see that the child receives suitable education. The LEA has, also, a duty to provide education.

EXCLUSION

When a headteacher excludes a pupil from school the parents must be informed as soon as possible about the length of the exclusion and the reason for it. Parents must also be informed if the headteacher intends to make an exclusion permanent, and be told that they may make representations to the LEA and the governing body.

If the headteacher excludes a pupil for a total of more than five days in any one term; or where, as a result of the exclusion, the pupil would lose the opportunity of taking a public examination; then the LEA and the governing body must be informed in writing, without delay, of the decision, the period of exclusion and the reasons for it.

Where the exclusion is permanent, or for more than five days in any one term, or the pupil would be prevented from taking public exams, the LEA must consult the governing body before they decide whether the pupil should be reinstated at once, or by a particular date, or not reinstated. If the exclusion is for an indefinite period, the governors take the decision about reinstatement. If the governors do not intend to direct the headteacher to reinstate the pupil, or if the LEA considers that the reinstatement should be at an earlier date, the LEA can direct the headteacher to reinstate immediately, or at a fixed date, although the LEA must consult the governors about this.

APPEALS

Parents must be informed that they have a right of appeal to the governors, and that they may also appeal to an appeal committee if the governors do not agree that the pupil is to be reinstated. These appeal committees have been set up in every area, and governors are often invited to serve on them, though not to hear cases in which they have been involved as governors.

If the pupil and parents are to appear before the governors, it is essential that they receive a fair hearing. It may be desirable for them to be advised and accompanied by a 'friend', as teachers have a right to be. Some LEAs recommend that, at the end of the hearing, the headteacher and any other governor directly involved with the case, withdraw, or at least abstain from voting.

When you have to consider an appeal against exclusion, there are a number of aspects you should bear in mind:

- A headteacher must be able to bar a pupil from school, or send them home at once, if their behaviour causes serious problems, or if they have a contagious infection.
- The school must be able to function properly while problems are being resolved.
- The child's education should be disrupted as little as possible.
- These problems need to be dealt with as quickly as possible.

In addition to hearing about the immediate reason for exclusion, governors should be told about past problems, and steps taken to resolve them. This will include consultation and discussion with parents, and may include the involvement of the education welfare service, or other agencies such as social work departments if the child, or family, are known to them.

CAUSES OF PROBLEMS

Problems can arise because parents do not respond to invitations to come to school to discuss their child's behaviour, or because they find that they cannot exercise the control that they have promised.

Many exclusions of which governors are informed are 'for the record'. The pupil is already back in school, or has been transferred elsewhere, with the agreement of the parents. You should satisfy yourself that suitable steps have been taken to see that the child's education is not harmed, and that the work of other pupils is not disrupted. In some areas, the governors, or a sub-committee of the board, meet the pupil and parents, receive reports and discuss the matter in detail. In other areas, only appeals against exclusion are referred to the governors.

Problems may arise with a pupil because of the way in which the school operates, or because of a poor relationship with a member of staff. It may be no one's 'fault'. Schools will usually try to resolve such problems before they become a matter for the governors, by placing the pupil in a different teaching group, or adjusting that pupil's curriculum, where possible. Governors should find out what steps have been taken already.

If no solution can be found within the school, a change of school may meet the difficulty, if parents will accept this. If that is not possible, it may be necessary to arrange a period of education at home or in a residential school. Neither is a satisfactory conclusion, either educationally, socially or financially, but one pupil cannot be allowed to disrupt the work of others. If a relationship with a teacher is the cause of the problem, the headteacher should tell governors what advice has been given to the teacher in an attempt to resolve the problem.

SCHOOL RULES

Although a meeting to consider an exclusion is not the place to do so, you should find out about the system for dealing with discipline problems at your school:

- What are the school rules? Have governors discussed and approved them?
- What support do teachers have, if they have problems with discipline?
- What other sanctions are tried first? How do they work?

You might also want to ask:

- Does one teacher have particular problems in keeping order?
- Are there similar problems in neighbouring schools? Is there a social problem in the district, which the school cannot remedy, but on which the governors could make representations?

Annual parents' meeting

Not less than two weeks after sending out the annual report to parents, the governors must hold a meeting for them, unless there are special reasons why this is not possible. At the meeting, parents may ask questions about the report and the work of the governors, and also about the running of the school, and what the LEA has done. Governors may have to try to answer all the questions, if there is no officer of the LEA present.

If the number of parents present is equal to, or more than, one fifth of the number of registered pupils at the school, they may pass resolutions, which may be directed to the governors, the headteacher or the LEA. The governors must consider any such resolutions or pass them on to the appropriate person. They must also report back at the next annual meeting on these resolutions. For a school with 100 children on roll, 20 parents need to be present to pass a resolution. But even if there are not enough present for this, you should take note of any points raised by parents. Of course, if you do take action, you do not need to wait a year to tell parents that you have done so.

All parents of registered pupils are entitled to attend and vote. The headteacher may also attend, but not vote. The only other people entitled to attend are those whom the governors have invited, and they may not vote. So if the press turns up, or anyone else uninvited, you can ask them to leave.

It is worth giving some thought to encouraging attendance at the meeting. Your letter of invitation, which goes out with the annual report, should aim to be friendly. If the school is able to arrange some attraction, such as a display by pupils, and to offer a cup of tea, this is helpful. Some schools have gone much further than this, and organised a whole day of activities for the whole family, with the annual meeting as one event.

The meeting will usually be chaired by the chairman of governors, and the other governors may like to mingle with the audience.

Neither the annual meeting nor the election of parent governors is a function of the parent-teacher association or home-school association, but the PTA should encourage parents to attend.

Building plans

You may be asked to consider plans for an extension to or replacement of your school buildings. Do make sure that the staff, teaching and non-teaching, are fully consulted. Look at access, safety, the position of electric points, the height of windows, and try to image how the building will appear to people who are to work in it. The plans may involve the removal of part of the building. Can this be done without disruption? Will it be safe for pupils, or will the work area have to be fenced off? Will the building involve noise and dust which could disrupt teaching? Will playground space be lost?

'Opting out'

Any discussion about 'opting out' or becoming 'grant maintained' will involve careful consideration by the governors, and will certainly require special meetings.

Secondary schools, and primary schools with more than 300 pupils will, from September 1989, be able to apply to leave the control of the LEA and become 'grant maintained', with funds received directly from the government. Governors may apply for such a change, but must first hold a secret ballot of parents, at which a simple majority of those who vote must agree to the proposal to 'opt out'. The parents can start the process themselves, and if 20 per cent request it, the governors must hold a ballot, as above. If fewer than 50 per cent of all parents take part in the voting, a further ballot must be held within 14 days. The result of the second ballot will be binding on the governors, whatever percentage of parents vote. It will be important to remember this when fixing the date of the first ballot. The secretary of state for education and science will have the power to refuse a request to opt out if he believes that there is insufficient support for the idea among the parents.

If a school becomes grant maintained, a new governing body will be set up, and the governors will have all the responsibility for running it, not just the powers they will have under local management schemes. They will not be able to call upon the free services of the LEA for in-service training, advice, central purchasing arrangements, repairs, extensions or many other aspects which schools now take for granted. They may instead have to pay commercial firms for services at present supplied by the LEA. Schools which opt out will not be able to change their status at once – for example from comprehensive to grammar – and cannot apply to 'opt back' to LEA control and financing for 10 years.

Charges for school activities

At present some LEAs charge, or permit schools to charge, for some things, which other LEAs supply free. These include swimming lessons, individual music tuition, materials for cooking, needlework and other crafts, coaching for sports activities and field trips.

In future governors may be asked to decide whether there should be charges and if so, at what level, and whether there should be exemptions for those whose parents cannot pay.

Where such a charge is proposed, governors may decide to hold a special meeting to consider all the relevant points, and to draw up a scale of charges and exemptions.

11
Different schools

Church schools

If you are a governor of a church school, you may find that you have more responsibilites, and that school government is looked at differently. Aided schools, in particular, may look more to the diocesan education board than the LEA. Their governors will have more responsibilities for the care of the premises for which the parish or other body has to supply 15 per cent of costs. Governors have more responsibility for appointing staff, issuing the information about the school to parents, organising the election of the parent governors, and other duties which, in county and controlled schools, are carried out by the LEA. If the school is 'endowed', the governors may be the trustees of funds. In aided schools, too, there are fewer elected parent governors, but their number is made up by one of the foundation governors being a parent.

Aided and controlled schools must still comply with the same laws and requirements as county schools in regard to the education of pupils, although there may be variations in the curriculum, and perhaps in the dates of some holidays. Parents of pupils may still choose to withdraw their children from religious education and worship, and governors may wish to know what alternative arrangements are made for these pupils.

Many village schools are church schools, catering for all the local population, so it should never be assumed that all parents and pupils, or the staff, are churchgoers.

If the governors of an aided or special agreement school pass a resolution to alter the nature of the school, or to discontinue it, they must hold another meeting not less than 28 days later, and consider the matter again. If the LEA proposes to make any changes to the status of these schools, they must consult the governors first.

Grouped schools

There are still a few areas where two or more schools are grouped under one governing body. These will usually be primary schools serving the same area: for example, an infant and junior school. You may wish to press your LEA to end this system, and to give each school its own board of governors. Each school should have parent and teacher representatives on the governing body, and each headteacher should attend. It is obviously more difficult to discuss the business of two or more schools, and headteachers have been known to be reluctant to air all their problems before the headteachers of neighbouring schools. It may be easier to concentrate on one school at each meeting, while dealing with each headteacher's report each time. This may be easier if the meeting is held in the school receiving particular consideration. Governors should try to maintain an interest in and visit each school.

Boarding schools

Where over half the pupils of a school are boarders, it may not be possible to hold parent elections, and the governors may simply appoint parents as governors. There will be extra responsibilities in watching over the needs and provisions of the school for resident pupils and staff. If the school has both boarding and day pupils, the needs of both should be remembered. It may not be possible to hold an annual meeting for parents, but the annual report must still be produced, and distributed.

Special schools

These are schools for children who have special mental, physical or emotional needs. The ratio of teachers to pupils will be higher, and there may be medical auxiliaries and other non-teaching staff employed at the school, or visiting regularly. The boards of such schools have to include a person from the voluntary organisation which the LEA considers most clearly linked with the needs of the pupils.

If the school serves a large region, there may be difficulties about electing parent governors and holding an annual meeting, and the arrangements noted above for boarding schools would then apply.

If you are a governor of a special school, you may want to consider the following:

- Is the physical provision adequate and well-maintained – for example, ramps, handrails, and other special facilities?
- Is the curriculum adequate? Are pupils given an opportunity to try things for themselves, or are they over-protected?
- Does the LEA provide general, as well as specialised, in-service training courses?
- Are there any links with local mainstream schools, for pupils and staff?
- How are pupils prepared for life after school?

Hospital schools

Here again it may be difficult, with a changing population of pupils who are patients, to organise parent elections, or hold an annual meeting. Governors may appoint, instead, the parent of a child registered at the school, or a person who has one or more children of school age. In all the cases where governors appoint the parents, the persons must not be elected or co-opted members of the LEA, or employees of the LEA, or of the governors of an aided school maintained by the LEA.

Governors will want to be sure that conditions for teaching are as convenient as possible within a hospital setting:

- How are links with a pupil's own school maintained?
- What happens about the education of a child who may be in and out of hospital several times, with periods at home in between hospital stays?
- What special equipment is needed – computers, bed desks, etc – and is there other equipment which would help?
- Is it possible to enlist the help of parents?
- Could local secondary schools help?

Campus schools

Where a local authority has grouped a number of educational (and perhaps other) facilities on one site, there may, in the past, have been one governing body for all the facilities. These may include, in addition to the school, a youth centre, adult centre, sports facilities, public library, clinic, and so on. The governors are now responsible only for the school, but the LEA may have set up an overall 'managing board', of which the school governors are a part. How the meetings and responsibilities of the governors fit into this will depend on local arrangements.

Nursery schools

The Acts do not require there to be governors for nursery schools, but as these have operated successfully in the past, many LEAs will continue to set them up. They do not have to conform to the same limits on membership and function as schools for children of school age, but the LEA will set out the details in the instrument and articles.

Sixth-form and tertiary colleges

Many young people over 16 now receive their education in these colleges. In the past, tertiary colleges have been governed under further education governing regulations, and sixth-form colleges under secondary school governing arrangements. With the restrictions on numbers now applied to schools, LEAs may seek different patterns for sixth-form colleges in future, since, like nursery schools, these colleges cater for people of non-statutory school age. No one under 18 will be able to be a governor of either type of college, but you should find out what local pattern there is if you are a governor of a sixth-form college.

Because of the restriction on people under 18 being governors, it is important that the governors arrange to hear the views of students themselves, rather than receiving these at second-hand, through parents and teachers. You may wish to suggest that representative students be invited to attend as observers and be consulted where that is appropriate, or the headteacher might be asked to include a report from any student council or similar body.

12
Curriculum and Organisation

Curriculum

What is the curriculum? It is not just a list of the subjects on the timetable, but everything that affects what is taught and what is learned. So it encompasses homework and exam choices, table manners and school uniform, equal opportunities for all pupils, and positive discrimination for those who need it. It includes human relationships, racial equality and awareness, health and careers education, political and religious education.

What is the 'hidden curriculum'? Perhaps this can best be described as the attitudes and values which pupils pick up from the school.

THE NATIONAL CURRICULUM

Starting with pilot schemes in 1989, all pupils will study the 'national curriculum', although some exceptions may be made for pupils with learning problems. The national curriculum will consist of a core of subjects – maths, English and science – which all pupils will study throughout their period of compulsory education, from 5 to 16. To these will be added the foundation subjects – history, geography, technology, art, music and physical education. Religious education is already required in every school. At secondary school, all pupils will also study a modern language. In Wales, Welsh will be either a core or foundation subject, although schools in Wales can apply not to teach Welsh.

About 70 per cent of school time will be taken up by core and foundation subjects, leaving about one and half school days for other subjects. How will your school fit in everything else, including religious education? How will the staffing of the school be affected by these changes?

From 1989, too, national standards of attainment are to be set, with the first examinations of them in 1991. All pupils will be tested at the age of 7, and again at 11, 14 and 16. The results will be published, for the school, if not for individual pupils. Governors will have to monitor the results, and report on them to parents in their annual report.

MONITORING

As governors, you have to monitor what is provided. The way in which it is delivered is a matter for the professional staff. Governors do not choose the textbooks or set the exams, but you should certainly keep an eye on the way in which the curriculum is put over to the pupils, and the results. For example, in secondary schools:

- How is the homework timetable planned?
- How many hours of homework a week are children of different ages expected to complete?
- Is homework marked?
- How are pupils and parents prepared for making choices of exam subjects?
- Do all pupils, black and white, girls and boys, have equal opportunities to study any aspect of the curriculum, or is, say, music only available to a limited group? Is woodwork limited to less able pupils or only to boys?
- Do all pupils have a full programme of careers education?

Similarly in the primary school:

- What additional help is available for those who have problems in learning to read?
- Are there library books which explore a wide variety of situation, or do they all describe white middle-class family life?

In all schools:

- What use is made of neighbourhood facilities, and parents for visits, talks and demonstrations?
- Are the governors ever invited to take part in visits, etc?

You cannot demand or expect the right of entry to a teacher's lessons, but you could ask if this could be arranged. You could find out about the teacher's conditions of service, how their time is allocated, and what they do on a voluntary basis.

- To what extent is the curriculum affected by the availability of teachers able to teach it?

- Is the curriculum affected at all by the presence in the school of large numbers of children from ethnic minority backgrounds?
- If your school is 'all white', how are the pupils prepared for living in a multi-ethnic society which they are not, at present, experiencing?
- How is the curriculum affected by local employment?
- To what extent do the requirements of higher education affect the curriculum?
- What curricular links are there between schools – sharing the teaching of the minority subjects, for example – and between secondary schools and their contributory primary schools, or between primary schools and local nursery schools and play-groups?

PRIMARY AND SECONDARY

While the national curriculum will in future set the framework of subjects which children are to be taught, and national tests will measure what they have learned, the curriculum in secondary schools may offer clearer opportunities for governors to ask questions than does the curriculum in primary schools.

In the infant and first school, children are learning about co-operation and friendship, especially those who have not had the benefit of nursery school. They are learning to use their bodies, as well as their minds, in ways which may be new to them; both whole-body movements, such as walking along a form, forward rolls, jumping over a rope; and fine movements, such as using their eyes to follow movements, their fingers to shape letters, their hands to form clay or express meaning.

They are learning to use tools – pencils, paintbrushes, scissors – and materials – paper, cloth and card.

They are learning social behaviour – not only politeness, but sharing and helping, tidying up after an activity, contributing to a class display, relationships with non-family adults and with authority.

They are learning self-confidence, to speak up in front of others, to take on small tasks, to ask questions, even to be leaders.

While many of these new skills will contribute to their intellectual development, they will not be skills which can be tested, but they are essential life skills.

As children progress through school, they acquire other skills: telling the time, road safety, how to use the telephone, where local services are to be found, as well as reading and writing skills. Children do not enter school equally well-equipped. Some can recognise and name 10 colours; others cannot name any.

In the early years, teachers help to impart these 'life-skills' to their pupils, and these offer an opportunity for every child to do well, to earn praise and feel part of the group, even if they stumble over reading or mathematics.

The attitudes which adults show to children are a vital factor in children's learning, and this is something which an outsider, such as a visiting governor, may be better able to assess than those who work in the school. The 'feel', even the sounds and smell of a school, may tell you more about how learning is going on than any formal report.

Organisation

The way in which the school is organised is as much a part of curriculum arrangements as is the timetable.

In the early years at school, children may remain with one teacher for more than one year. They may be grouped strictly according to age, or there may be a loose grouping with some slightly older children with younger ones. This is often referred to as 'family grouping'. In the later years a group of children is more likely to be of similar age, although with falling numbers of pupils, and in small village schools, it may still be necessary for a teacher to take children from a wider range age-group than one year.

Children usually move on to the next stage of education together, even if to different schools. Whether the age is 11, 12, or 13, and the new school called secondary, high, comprehensive or some other name, there is sure to be a considerable difference in organisation to which children have to adjust. In the primary stage most teaching will have been given by one teacher to each group. There may be a change for games or music, but most of the basic education will have been in the hands of the class teacher. In the later stages of the primary school, or where there are middle schools, more specialist teachers may have been used. In the secondary school, each subject may have a different teacher, and the form teacher may not teach his or her class for any subject.

Secondary schools use a number of ways to organise themselves. Children may still remain in a class group with their peers, but may be split into other groups for teaching. Year groups may be combined into 'lower school' and 'upper school', with the lower forms in the school following a basic or foundation course and the upper forms following examination courses. This system may be adopted by schools which have to occupy 'split sites', where one part of the school is at some distance from another part.

Some schools, instead, adopt a vertical division, perhaps called 'houses', each of which is run like a small school. Pupils may be divided according to ability in bands or streams, or may be taught, for all or most subjects, in 'mixed-ability' groups. There are still schools in which a number of subjects are taught in single-sex groups. This is usual for games and physical education, but may also be extended to practical subjects, such as needlework and crafts.

Single-sex schools are more common at secondary level than primary, and governors may wish to take a particular interest in how pupils learn to work and co-operate with the other sex if these are not a part of the everyday environment of the school.

Some schools use the 'house' division to organise non-academic activities, such as sport, fund-raising and social activities. Find out how your school is organised, and if it is divided for administrative, teaching or other purposes.

13
Coping with Problems

Situations can arise when you, as a governor, have to tackle a serious problem. This chapter looks at some of the most likely ones such as:
- The headteacher is unable to communicate with his or her staff.
- A teacher takes time off repeatedly, for insufficient reason.
- The chairman of the governing body is biased.
- The LEA does not tackle repair problems urgently.
- The clerk is inefficient.
- The parents want you to sack a teacher.
- Another school is poaching your pupils.
- The school is constantly being vandalised.

Teachers   Every LEA will have procedures for dealing with staff who are not doing their job properly, and this applies to caretakers as well as headteachers. Remember that the LEA is the employer, and the most you can do is to make a recommendation, although the situation may change in the future if governors have greater powers when there will be even more need to walk warily in such matters. You are not immune from charges of defamation or wrongful dismissal. Governors must act in good faith if they are to be protected from the consquences of their decisions.

We have all, through our rates and taxes, invested a great deal of money in the training and employment of teachers. Teachers are human, like the rest of us; they have worries, problems and illnesses which may affect their work. They may be doing the job in the wrong place, or with the 'wrong' pupils. But local authority advisers and inspectors should be made aware if there is a problem. If it is the headteacher who is the problem, or, in excessive loyalty, refuses to see the problem with another member of staff, the governors may have to take action. Even then, it is, usually better if the whole matter is dealt with very discreetly, at least initially. The chairman should talk with the headteacher and local advisers. It may be that the problem can be resolved before it becomes public, since publicity could only be damaging for the school. A move to another position, further training and advice, even early retirement, may be solutions offered by the LEA. Governors should avoid stirring up conflict and encouraging local gossip, and try to ensure that some action is taken quickly.

A member of staff may have a complaint against the headteacher or another member of staff or the LEA, and the governors may have to adjudicate, if local grievance procedures involve the governors. Your articles will make clear what are the procedures when the dismissal of a headteacher or other member of staff is contemplated, and you should also have expert guidance from an LEA officer.

The chairman

The chairman is elected each year, so you have an opportunity to make a change at the first meeting of the school year. Send a nomination in writing, properly proposed and seconded, with the agreement of the candidate, well before the date of the meeting, to your clerk. This overcomes any embarrassment or difficulty in suggesting a second name, if the present chairman has already been proposed.

If there are problems at the meeting, and it seems that a majority of the governors feel that the chairman is seriously biased, or has gone astray, you could propose a vote of 'no confidence' in the chairman.

Your clerk or LEA officer should be able to indicate to the chairman if he or she is acting wrongly.

Problems arise if the chairman, as sometimes happens, seems to be opposed to one governor, or a small group. This may be the parents or the teacher governors. Such a situation must not be allowed to continue. The vice-chairman could be asked to speak to the chairman, or the clerk or the headteacher may be willing to do so. Since the chairman controls the meeting, and acts for governors between meetings, it is obvious that there must be mutual trust and respect.

The local authority

The most usual problem encountered by governors is delay in carrying out repairs, or replying to governors' requests and resolutions. In the latter case, one of the LEA representatives on the board, especially any councillor, should be asked to chase up the matter. Your clerk may be able to help. If none of these succeeds, and the matter is urgent, governors may need to take other steps.

If the health and safety of pupils is endangered, you must not hesitate to exert strong pressure for defects to be remedied. You could call in the environmental health officer or the dangerous structures inspector. If there are traffic or security problems, ask the police for help; if fire hazards, ask the fire brigade to advise. If all else fails, it may be necessary to resort to threats of more drastic action. Like the heavy artillery, these actions are best kept in reserve for the most serious needs, when nothing else has brought results.

The main threats you might have to use are:
- to inform parents of the hazard, and seek their support in lobbying councillors. A number of letters to local councillors from worried parents can be very effective
- to inform the press about the situation. No one likes adverse publicity, but consider whether such action would damage the school in future
- to close the school, or part of it, and send the pupils home
- to write to your MP
- to complain to the secretary of state for education and science, under Section 67 (1) of the 1944 Education Act, on the grounds that the LEA is not carrying out its duty properly.

Except in the most extreme circumstances, such threats are not put into practice. The mere threat may gain the action you want, so use them sparingly. A non-functioning and unrepaired boiler may be a reasonable complaint. An unrepaired lock on a cupboard is not. The LEA has the power to remove its nominees if they act irresponsibly.

The clerk

If your clerk is inefficient, or fails to attend the meetings, or otherwise causes problems for the board, or if you cannot find someone willing to act as clerk, you can ask the

LEA to appoint another person, and for a county school they must do so. The LEA must consult you if they plan to change your clerk, other than at your request.

Other schools

If your school appears to be losing favour with local parents, who are choosing to send their children elsewhere, try to find out why this is happening. It may be local rumours about your school. Are they true? If so, try to take steps to remedy the complaint. If not, take steps to scotch the rumours, and give your school a good press.

OPEN ACCESS

If you are losing pupils because another school is taking abnormal steps to attract them, you could complain to the LEA, although with the new system of open access this may be ineffective. From September 1989 for secondary schools, and later for primary schools, schools will be required to operate an open-access system, and admit pupils up to their 'standard number' if there is a demand for places. The 'standard number' will be the number that the school could have admitted in 1979, unless conditions have changed considerably since then, for example, by the demolition of part of the buildings. The aim is for more parents to be able to place their child in the school of their first choice (unless it is a selective school).

There will be problems for schools, both those which receive an influx of pupils, and those which lose pupils, so some schools may recruit by taking unusual steps.

You may have to take similar steps to ensure the popularity of your school. Sometimes, the ethnic make-up of the school is the unspoken reason for one group of parents choosing to send their children elsewhere. If you recognise this is so for your school, try to ensure that the curriculum is so developed that all the pupils can receive a properly balanced education which is not distorted in favour of any one section or aspect. You may discover, from talking with parents, staff or pupils, where there is dissatisfaction with an aspect of the school, which could be the root cause of problems. Any such enquiry has to be undertaken very carefully, and it may be better to ask people what improvements could be suggested, rather than what is wrong with present arrangements. Parent and staff governors may be able to indicate some areas which are causing concern.

If yours is a very popular school, you may be full to capacity, and unable to admit all who wish to come. The governors may have to decide who is to be admitted and who rejected. The basis should be worked out to be as fair as possible, and the criteria for admission should be made known. This may not stop parents moving house or attending a local church in order to gain a place in your school. Open access may give you more problems, but it may be possible for the boards of several schools to work together to plan an equitable share of available pupils for each school, given goodwill by all concerned.

Vandalism

If your school has a particular problem, try to find out who is causing it and what steps are being taken. If it is pupils at the school, what is the school doing to alter attitudes? If the problems arise from others in the neighbourhood, can the police help? Some schools have been able to organise, with the help of the police, 'schools watch' schemes, where neighbours of the school keep an eye on the premises, and report those seen causing damage.

If the pupils are encouraged to take a pride in the school, if repairs are carried out quickly, if graffiti is removed at once, if parents back up the school's efforts, and if the governors take an interest in seeing that the school is kept in good condition, it may be easier to overcome the problem.

Sometimes rivalry with another school leads to damage. The

headteachers and governors of both schools should try to take urgent action to bring the rivalry to an end.

Where the culprits are known, action should always be taken, either by prosecuting them, or by disciplinary action in the school. Anti-social behaviour which remains uncondemned and unpunished may only encourage others.

Closures and amalgamations

If your school is one which is scheduled for closure or amalgamation, the LEA must keep you fully informed. You should find out, in the case of closure:

- What arrangements are to be made for the future education of children from the area at present served by your school?
- What arrangements are being made for staff?
- If closure is to be gradual (no more children to be admitted, but those already there to complete their time at school), how will a full curriculum be maintained as the numbers fall?

If your school is to be amalgamated with another school, find out:

- If some pupils are to transfer to another school, how will they be integrated into the other schools?
- How is this to be done? Will children remain with their friends?
- What steps are being taken to harmonise the curriculum and teaching methods of the two schools?

In either case, find out:

- What is to happen to the school building?
- Whether transport arrangements to the new school from your area are satisfactory?

You may wish to fight the proposals. If so, you will need to gather all the facts about the other school as well as your own, and look at the pattern of school provision across the district. This is not the place to describe how to run a campaign of this sort, but, at each stage, consider your decision again. On the one hand, school buildings are expensive to maintain, and one comfortably full school is much cheaper than two half-empty ones. On the other hand, there may be particular reasons to oppose the closure – if your school is in a village, and provides a community focal point, for example. You will need the support of the local community, especially parents, and you may wish to establish a committee to consider all aspects and to run your campaign. It is probably better if this is not done directly by the governors.

Bullying and racism

If there are problems of pupils behaving aggressively towards each other, you must find out what steps are being taken to check this.

- Does the organisation and curriculum positively encourage good relations?
- Are parents involved if their child is an offender?
- Is there anything else which can be tried?

Parents

Parents now have a larger share in deciding about the school, so you need to encourage them to become involved. Governors can play a big part in this encouragement. Booklets of the Home and School Council are written to help parents and schools to understand each other better, and to encourage participation. If there is no Home-School Association, the National Confederation of Parent-Teacher Associations can advise on starting one. PTAs are not solely fund-raising groups, although most schools will welcome that sort of help. They also help parents to understand what happens in school, and how they can help their children to benefit from their education.

If parents seem uninterested in the school, and do not support events or respond to invitations, governors should be concerned to find out why.

- If there is a home-school association or PTA, are those involved mainly from one part of the area, or one 'class'?
- How are invitations worded? Is the school warm and welcoming, or is it difficult to find the way in, or to know where to go, once inside?
- Do you need to produce your school booklet and annual report in a different way, and in another language?

There are many ways to encourage parents to come to school and to take part, but much depends on the attitude of the headteacher and staff.

Whether or not you encounter problems, being a governor is a demanding task. Whether it is also rewarding, in terms of satisfaction with a job well done, a service freely given to the local community, for the benefit of present and future generations of children, will depend very much on the time, effort and interest which you are prepared to give.

Further Information

If you want to read more about any of the aspects covered by this book, try to find books written recently, as anything on governing published before 1988 may be out of date. You may like to join an organisation, or subscribe to a specialist magazine. *The Guardian* and the *Independent* publish weekly sections on education.

Magazines

School Governors, quarterly, by subscription of £14 a year, from 73 All Saints Road, Kings Heath, Birmingham B14 7LN.
Times Educational Supplement, weekly from newsagents.
Education, weekly from newsagents.

Books

Kenneth Brooksbank and Keith Anderson, *School Governors*, 2nd ed, Longman, 1988.
Peter Harding, *A Guide to Governing Schools*, Harper and Row, 1987.
Joan Sallis, *Schools, Parents and Governors*, Routledge, 1988.
Felicity Taylor, *Parents Rights in Education*, Longman, 1986.
Elizabeth Wallis, *Education A-Z: where to look things up, sources on major educational topics*, 5th ed, Advisory Centre for Education, 1988.
London Diocesan Board, *Schools for the Future: Comments on the 1988 Bill*, NAGM Distribution, 31 Forsyth House, London SW1V 2LE.

National Foundation for Educational Research, *Governors' Reports and Annual Parents' Meetings*, NFER, 1988.

Official Publications

A New Partnership for Our Schools (The Taylor Report), HMSO, 1977. The Education Acts of 1980, 1981, 1986 and 1988, all from HMSO.

Equal Opportunities Commission, *Equal Opportunities and the School Governor*, free leaflet from Equal Opportunities Commission, 1 Bedford Street, London WC2E 9HD.

Helpful Organisations

National Association of Governors and Managers (NAGM), 81 Rustlings Road, Sheffield S11 7AB Subscription £5 a year for individuals. Publishes a termly journal, many useful papers of guidance for governors, and training materials. Has branches in some areas, and holds conferences and training sessions.

Campaign for the Advancement of State Education (CASE)
The Grove, High Street, Sawston, Cambridge CB2 4HJ
Publishes *Parents and Schools*. Branches in many areas.

Action for Governors Information and Training (AGIT)
c/o Community Education Development Council, Briton Road, Coventry CV2 4LF.
Lists training resources for governors, and holds conferences.

Advisory Centre for Education (ACE)
18 Victoria Park Square, London E2 9PB. Publishes *ACE Bulletin* six times a year. £7.50 subscription.

Home amd School Council, 81 Rustings Road, Sheffield S11 7AB. Subscription £3 a year. Publishes, each term, a booklet on some aspects of home/school relations.

Training

In addition to your LEA and the National Association of Governors and Managers (NAGM), training may be provided in your area by political parties, diocesan boards of education, CASE, or the Workers' Educational Association (WEA). See your local phone directory to contact these organisations, or write to the addresses given above, for national organisations.

Appendix 1
Composition of governing bodies following the 1986 (No.2) Education Act

County primary schools	No. of pupils			
	Under 100	100–299	300–599	Over 600
LEA governors	2	3	4	5
Parent governors	2	3	4	5
Teacher governors	1	1	2	2
Headmaster	1	1	1	1
Primary schools in area of a minor authority				
Minor authority governor	1	1	1	1
Co-opted governors	2	3	4	4
Other primary schools/ secondary schools				
Co-opted governors	3	4	5	5

Voluntary/controlled schools	No. of pupils			
	Under 100	100–299	300–599	Over 600
LEA governors	2	3	4	5
parent governors	2	3	4	5
Teacher governors	1	1	2	2
Headteacher	1	1	1	1

Primary schools in area of a minor authority

Minor authority governor	1	1	1	1
Foundation governors	2	3	4	4
Co-opted governors	0	0	0	1

Other primary schools/ secondary schools

Foundation governors	2	3	4	4
Co-opted governors	1	1	1	2

Aided and special agreement schools

LEA governors	At least one
Elected parent governors	At least one
Teacher governors	If under 300 on roll, at least one
	If over 300, at least two
Headteacher	If the head chooses to be a governor, but to be counted as one when determining the number of foundation governors

Primary school in the area of a minor authority

Minor authority	At least one
Foundation governors	To outnumber the other governors by 2, if the total number of governors is 18 or fewer, and by 3 if the total is over 18. One of the foundation governors must be the parent of a child registered at the school.

Other governors may be added
Provisions for voluntary schools start from 1 September 1989.

Maintained special schools
These have the same categories and numbers of governors as primary and secondary schools, but, except for hospital schools, must have one (if under 100 pupils) or 2 (100+ pupils) governors appointed by appropriate voluntary organisations, in place of co-options.

Hospital schools also have one governor nominated by the district health authority.

Appendix 2 Extract from a Primary Headteacher's Report

This fictitious report may help governors to think about the kind of questions they want to raise.

Staff

We started the new school with a full complement of staff. Mr Daw joined us as a redeployed teacher, as his former school has closed. he has special skills with children who are slow learners. Miss Osprey is a probationer teacher, and I have asked Mrs Swallow to supervise her probationary period.

Were any governors involved in the appointments? How are the new staff settling in? How many slow learners do we have?

My deputy, Mr Martin, has been appointed to a headship, and will take up his new post in January.

What arrangements are being made to appoint a new deputy?

The outbreak of summer flu last term affected staff as well as pupils, and I had difficulty in securing adequate cover at short notice. We were able to cover all classes, but had to cancel sports day, and two planned outings.

Why were there problems in obtaining cover? Was this a widespread problem? Have the visits been rearranged?

Mr Gull, our caretaker, attended a course of training for caretakers, and although we had help from the caretaker of a neighbouring school during his absence, this was less than the full cover which the office promised to send us.

Should we protest about lack of cover for both teachers and caretaker?

Pupils
As in recent years, our intake of new pupils was well below our standard number. Governors will recall that demolition of housing in the area has been the main reason. We understand from the housing office that the new housing will be available for letting to families from November, when we expect to see our numbers rise.

Will the standard number of the school be reviewed when numbers increase? What liaison will there be with the schools of pupils who are moving into the district? Will numbers rise so that we need extra teachers?

At the end of last term, 38 pupils left the school. 25 went to the local comprehensive, and 5 to other secondary schools on parental option, one after an appeal by parents. Five pupils left the district on rehousing, and 3 children, in one family, went back to Pakistan.

What liaison was there with secondary schools before pupils transferred?

One pupil who left last term has been praised by the police for his help in telling them about some vandalising of new houses in the area.

Perhaps the governors would like to add their congratulations?

One child, who caused us worry last year by her behaviour problems, has been placed in the care of the local authority, while still attending here.

Are there many children who are 'at risk' in the school? Does a member of staff

We have good relations with her social worker, problems have been fewer this term, and the child seems happier.

have a responsibility for liaising with social workers?

Attendance

After the absences caused by summer flu last term, we have an excellent record for this term so far. One family of two children has caused concern by lateness, and some parent-condoned absence. I have asked the welfare officer to treat this as a priority, as we had problems with this family when we had another child, a few years ago. The office say staff shortages may mean there will be a delay, as there is a lot of work with secondary-age pupils at present.

Does the welfare department not consider primary absences to be important? Has the school been able to give any help?

Education developments

Our recent 'Baker day' was spent at the Education Computer Centre, studying how to make the best use of our computer facilities. Mr Falconer has worked with staff at the centre on a programme to develop our environmental studies, and other schools are keen to make use of this programme, too.

Will governors be able to see the programme? Is there any financial reward for the teacher or the school?

The new sex-education programme, approved by the governors last term, has now been introduced. Parents have been invited to see the films and books in the school library which are used to support this programme.

May governors see the film? What were the parents' reactions?

Glossary of Educational Terms

Compiled by Elizabeth Wallis
of the Advisory Centre for Education (ACE)

Advisers   Teachers who give general or subject advice to schools, develop facilities for their subjects, and organise in-service training programme. Sometimes called local inspectors.

AEO   Area education officer. Many LEAs divide their territories into areas or divisions for administrative purposes.

Agreed syllabus   Non-denominational programme of religious education adopted by LEAs for use in schools.

Aided school   see Voluntary school.

Allowances   Under the Teachers' Pay and Conditions Act 1987, a new pay structure came into operation. Scale posts were abolished and incentive allowances were introduced. The number of these A and B allowances depends upon the group size of the school.

Ancillary staff   Clerical, welfare, technical, caretaking or supervisory staff in schools.

Articles of government   Set out the powers and duties of governors.

Assembly   Collective worship attended by school pupils. May also be used by teachers to demonstrate work carried out in classrooms, and to convey information on school activities.

Assessment   Measuring and evaluating skills, capabilities and limitations. Methods include tests and examinations. For children with special needs medical, social, psychological and other factors may also be used. For procedures for formal assessment of children with special needs, consult the Education Act 1981.

Assessment centre   Used to observe children who may have educational and social needs. Investigation over several months for children with special needs attending full or part-time.

Assisted places scheme Provision in the 1980 Education Act for pupils to attend independent schools, without being charged tuition or examination fees, which will be met by the government.

'At risk' register Individual schools list children identified by social services who are, or may be, in danger of emotional, physical and sexual abuse or mental cruelty from within their families.

Attendance officer *see* Educational social worker (ESW)

Attendance order Parents who are not sending their children to school, or 'otherwise' educating them, may have action taken against them by the LEA by the issuing of an order which may lead to legal action. *see also* Parent-condoned absence.

Baker days Under the Teachers Pay and Conditions Act 1987, five in-service training days a year for teachers in schools are compulsory. Named after Kenneth Baker, secretary of state for education and science, who piloted the Act through Parliament.

Banding The ability division of a year of pupils, each band containing several forms, which may then be streamed.

Basic skills Traditionally the three Rs – reading, writing and arithmetic.

BEC Business Education Council which approves and monitors courses in further education to replace former National Certificate and Diploma courses.

Bilateral school A secondary school which offers both academic and technical education.

Block timetabling Arrangements whereby a number of forms take a subject simultaneously, which facilitate both transfer of pupils between different teaching groups and team teaching.

Burnham scale The Burnham Committee, which formally negotiated teachers pay, was abolished by the Teachers' Pay and Conditions Act 1987. *see also* Allowances.

Campus A site on which are gathered a number of services – school clinic, library, etc may be included. Also the arrangement by which a number of educational provisions – e.g. school, youth club, adult centre – are grouped under a head of campus (usually the school head) for administrative purposes.

Capitation allowances An allowance allocated to each school to cover educational expenditure – e.g. books, stationery. Based on the number of children on the school roll, and taking their ages into account.

Careers service Advises young people and helps to place them in employment or a course for education and training. Operated by the LEA or the Department of Employment.

Cascade A method of in-service training: a few are trained then go and train others, who in their turn train others. May be used for governor training.

Catchment area A geographical area from which the LEA would like a school to draw most of its pupils. *see also* Choice of school.

CDT Craft, design and technology, a school curriculum subject.

CEO Chief education officer, or county education officer; sometimes called director of education or secretary for education.

Certificated teacher One qualified by completing a teacher training course (now three years plus a probationary year in a full-time teaching post).

Child-centred learning The focus is on the individual child's own interests rather than on the subject-matter.

Child guidance clinic A centre staffed by psychiatrists, educational psychologists and remedial teachers, for diagnosis and treatment of emotional problems and learning difficulties in children and young people. Part of the School Psychological Service.

Choice of school *see* Parental choice

Circular Policy statements issued by the DES to LEAs, which do not have the status of law.

City and Guilds Vocational foundation examinations set by the City and Guilds of London Institute.

City Technology Colleges The establishment in any urban area of a school with a technological bias, but following the national curriculum, for pupils between the age of 11 and 19. The education is free and pupils are selected. The Secretary of State may enter into agreement with any person or body to finance CTCs and may make grants towards the capital and/or running costs.

Cluster A group of secondary schools working together, perhaps on curriculum initiatives, and perhaps dividing the teaching of 16+ pupils between them.

Community governor Representatives chosen by elected parent, teacher and LEA-appointed governors. Such co-optees must also include a link between the local business community and the school.

Compensatory education Programme to help to reduce the intellectual and other handicaps for children growing up in deprived circumstances.

Comprehensive school Secondary school designed to educate children from the whole range of ability.

Continental day School day of one continuous session based on the German experience. The session might run from 8 am to 1 pm, with a half-hour break.

Continuing education   Belief that education is a life-long experience gained through formal and informal teaching.

Continuous assessment   Regular evaluation of course work. Marks achieved count towards final examination result.

Controlled school   *see* Voluntary school

Core curriculum   A group of subjects studied by all pupils.

Counsellor   An adviser in secondary schools on personal, academic and vocational problems. Usually it is a teacher with additional special training.

County school   A school owned and maintained by the LEA.

Criterion-referenced tests   Tests on a scale which measure an individual's performance against some absolute standard.

Day nursery   Operated by the social services department of the local authority. Accepts children from 0–5 for the whole day, when mothers are unable to care for them. A child-care centre, not an educational provision like a nursery class.

DEO   Divisional educational officer. Many LEAs divide their territories into areas or divisions for administrative purposes.

DES   Department of Education and Science, responsible for all education from nursery to higher and further education, and also adult education.

Development plan   A plan of all educational facilities, both existing and proposed, maintained by an LEA. Must be revised every five years and submitted to the secretary of state for approval. Frequently amended between revisions.

Discovery learning methods   Where children are enabled to learn for themselves rather than be told by the teacher.

Dyslexia   Used to describe the learning disorder of children who have difficulty in acquiring reading skills. Sometimes called word-blindness.

Educationally subnormal   Now obsolete term, originally used to describe children with an IQ below 70, who were sent to ESN (M) schools and below 50 to ESN(S) schools. Such children with moderate or severe learning difficulties are now described as 'children with learning difficulties'.

Educational psychologist   Professionally qualified and experienced teacher with a degree in psychology and post-graduate qualifications in educational psychology, who studies the intellectual, emotional, social and physical developments of children and young people.

Educational social worker   Formerly educational welfare officer. The ESW is employed to help with social problems. Visits homes, checks on absentees, etc in liaison with the school.

Emotional and behavioural disorders   Includes both neurotic and anti-social behaviour. Replaces the term 'maladjustment'.

Equal opportunities policy   A school's thinking and practice on gender, race, sexuality and disability.

Examinations   The main secondary school examinations are the General Certificate of Secondary Education (GCSE) taken at 16, and the General Certificate of Education (GCE) Advanced (A) Level, usually taken at 18. Scotland has its own examination system.

Exclusion   Debarment of pupil from school on disciplinary or medical grounds can be temporary, indefinite or permanent.

Falling rolls   The decline of the school population caused by the falling birth-rate.

Family grouping   The organisation of classes in primary schools so that the age-range extends over two or three years.

Field-study trips   Journeys undertaken by groups of students to enable them to gain first-hand practical experience in subjects such as geography, biology and environmental studies. May be a daily outing or a residential visit.

First schools   For children aged 5 to 8 or 9.

Flash cards   Cards with words or numbers printed to assist the teaching of reading and arithmetic.

Form entry (FE)   The number of forms (classes) which a school admits each year. A two FE infant school takes two classes (up to about 80 children) each year.

Foundation governors   Governors appointed by the foundation body of a voluntary school.

Foundation subjects   Subjects studied by all pupils.

Free school meals   As from April 1988, the discretion to provide free school meals was removed by the Social Security Act 1986. The only free meals which can now be provided are for children whose parents are on income support. It is up to the authority to decide what to provide.

Functional literacy   The ability to read and write sufficiently to cope with everyday life.

GCE   General Certificate of Education *see* Examinations.

GCSE General Certificate of Secondary Education *see* Examination.

Graded tests   Taken by pupils at a certain stage of proficiency rather than on a final examination basis.

Graduate   The holder of a degree. A graduate teacher must hold a post graduate certificate of education (PGCE), obtained after a year of further study.

Grant-maintained school   School financed directly from the DES after parents have voted to end LEA control, under the Education Reform Act 1988.

Grants   Mandatory and discretionary grants are available for courses in higher and further education. Applications for these are made through LEAs. School uniform grants are made under the 1944 Education Act. LEAs have the power to provide non-uniform clothing for any pupil who is unable to take advantage of his or her education because of inadequate or unsuitable clothing.

GRIDS   Guidelines for Review and Internal Development in Schools. A system used by staff to determine priorities for in-service training areas of the school to be reviewed by teachers.

Group (of a school)   Every school is placed in a group according to a 'Unit Total', calculated by the number and ages of children on the school roll. The group of the school determines the salary of the head and deputy head(s), and the number of points the school can allocate for appointments above main grade.

Group teaching   Breaking down a class into small groups of varying numbers within which children can proceed at their own pace or follow a particular line of interest.

HMI   Her Majesty's Inspector of Schools.

Home-school liaison teacher   Teacher responsible for working with parents of pupils who have special needs, and sometimes for maintaining the school's links with other services.

Home tuition   Teaching at home, or at a special centre, by a teacher employed by the LEA. Ten hours a week is the recommended minimum.

House   Subdivision of school, used mainly for sports competitions, though some large secondary schools use houses as units of school organisation to make internal administration more manageable, and to provide pastoral care. House usually contains whole age-range of school.

Humanities   Non-scientific and non-technical subjects, such as literature and history.

Induction period   Time allocated to familiarise a teacher with the organisation and procedures of the school.

Infant school   Catering for children between the ages of 5 and 7.

In-service training   Courses for practising teachers to enable them to update their skills. Since the passing of the Teachers Pay and Conditions Act 1987, five days in-service training for teachers in school is compulsory. Sometimes called 'Baker days'.

INSET   In-service education of teachers.

Inspector   see Adviser and HMI

Instrument of government   Sets out the constitution of the governing body and its working rules.

Integrated day   The planned use of the whole day for younger pupils, when they engage in all educational activities on an individual basis without a strict timetable.

Integration   The education of disabled and able-bodied children together in ordinary or mainstream schools.

Junior schools   Catering for pupils between the ages of 7 and 11.

LEA   Local education authorities. There are 104 LEAs in England and Wales.

Learning Difficulty   The capacity to acquire new skills at a slower rate than children of the same age. There are three levels – mild, moderate and severe.

Link course   A part-time course for school pupils in their final year, organised jointly by the school and a college of further education.

Local financial management   The delegation of the budget and finances of secondary schools and larger primary schools to the governors, introduced by the Education Reform Act 1988.

Main grade   Under the new pay structure brought about by the Teachers Pay and Conditions Act 1987, scale posts were abolished, and all teachers, with the exception of heads and deputy heads, are on a 'main scale'. This has 11 points, and teachers have been assimilated on to the scale according to their years of service.

Maintained school   Any school for whose running the LEA takes responsibility, both financial and administrative.

Major building project   A school building project costing more than £120,000 for voluntary schools and £200,000 for county schools, probably a new school or an extension to a school.

Middle school   Caters for children aged 8–12 or 9–13.

Minor building project   A school building project costing less than £120,000 for voluntary schools and £200,000 for county schools.

Minor local authority   A parish council, or a parish meeting if there is no parish council or, in their absence, the district council. The appointing body for one member of the governing body of a county primary school.

Mixed ability   A teaching group in which children of all abilities are taught together, not streamed or set. The usual way of teaching in primary schools, and common in the early years of secondary education.

Mode III   A method of assessing in which the syllabus and the method of assessment are decided by the school's teaching staff, and the assessing, whether by examination or other method, is carried out by the staff, though externally moderated.

Multi-cultural education   Catering for the needs of children from ethnic-minority groups. Education designed to ensure that all children are aware of/sensitive to our multi-cultural society. Also called multi-ethnic education.

National curriculum   Subjects prescribed by the secretary of state for education and science for teaching to all pupils in maintained schools (not independent schools) under the Education Reform Act 1988.

New maths   Curricula in mathematics for primary and/or secondary schools, with the emphasis on understanding the basic principles through practical work.

Non-maintained special schools   Non profit-making schools which operate under the Handicapped Pupils and Special Schools Regulations 1979. They may receive government grants and financial support from charities or trusts. Most pupils are placed in the schools by LEAs, which pay the fees.

Norm-referenced tests   Tests on which a score is interpreted by comparison with others, often to determine whether and by how much the score is better or worse than the average.

Nuffield maths and science   Curricula in maths and science, developed by teachers working on projects sponsored by the Nuffield Foundation. The emphasis is on discovery through practical experience. *see also* New maths.

Nursery class   A class in a state maintained school, which admits children from the age of 3.

Nursery school   Catering for 3–5 years old, full or part-time.

Nurture groups   Certain children deprived of normal relationships in early childhood may be placed in small groups to help compensate them socially and emotionally.

Observation centre   *see* Assessment centre

Open day   The school invites parents to inspect the work of their own children and the school in general. Teachers are available to talk to parents.

Open plan   A school building in which most or all of the teaching area is open, i.e. without internal walls.

Open enrolment   All schools must admit pupils up to the number they admitted in 1979–80, or the year immediately preceding the coming into force of the Education Reform Act 1988.

Opting out   Vote by parents to receive direct funding from the DES to end LEA control over the school. *see also* Grant-maintained school

Outreach   Provision of expert help in another setting, i.e. staff from special schools offering a service to ordinary schools.

Paired reading   Teaching a child to read with a fluent reader, usually the parent. Hence Parent Assisted Instruction in Reading.

Parental choice   The 1980 Education Act requires LEAs and governors to admit children to the school of parental preference, unless that would prejudice the provisions of efficient education or efficient use of resources; would be incompatible with selection arrangements for non-comprehensive schools. To be further extended by the 'open access' clauses of the 1988 Act.

Parent-condoned absence   Pupils' non attendance at school with the knowledge and/or encouragement of parents.

Parents' consultative council   Organisation established by an LEA for representative parent governors to inform, discuss and give views on educational policy making.

Peripatetic teacher   A teacher who teaches in a number of schools, e.g. a teacher of a musical instrument, or one who teaches individual children at home.

Playgroup   Registered with the social services department, but often assisted by the education department. Many groups affiliate to the Pre-School Playgroups Association (PPA).

Pre-school education   Different types of education for under-fives. Includes nursery schools, nursery classes and pre-school playgroups.

Probationary year   First year of service during which a teacher proves his/her practical efficiency, and so becomes a qualified teacher.

Profiling   An open system of recording pupils' personal achievement in all areas of activity. Used to supplement formal examination results.

Programmed learning   Step by step, self-correcting, individualised system of studying specific subjects, either in book form or with teaching machines.

Project   A topic studied by pupils individually and collectively with the class.

PTA   Parent-teacher association. A school-based association of parents and teachers. Its purpose is to facilitate home/school contacts and to work for the benefit of the school, often by raising funds. Sometimes used for other groups, such as parent association, or guild, or home and school society.

Pupil/teacher ratio   In a given school, the number of pupils divided by the total number of full-time staff (or their part-time equivalent), which in DES statistics include the head.

Pyramid   A secondary school and its contributory primary schools.

Qualified teacher   A certificated teacher or a graduate. New graduates becoming teachers are required to have a post-graduate certificate of education (PGCE).

Rate-support grant   Government grant aid to local authorities. It is calculated for each authority on a complex formula which involves population, density, age-structure, rateable value, etc. and is given in a lump sum, which the authorities then apportion at their own discretion.

Reading age   A child's score on standardised reading tests, worked out on the basis of average scores for each age.

Reception class   The first-year class of an infant school.

Religious education   The only compulsory subject for a school curriculum required by the 1944 Education Act. Parents have a right to withdraw their children on grounds of conscience.

Religious worship   Schools must provide a daily act of worship wholly or mainly of a broadly Christian character. It need not be at the beginning of the day, and it need not involve all pupils at the same time. *see also* Assembly.

Remedial class or department   Remedial teaching is designed to help pupils who have special difficulties. These classes or groups are organised where possible under the supervision of a specially trained teacher. Children may be withdrawn from some lessons for extra tuition in other subjects, or kept in a group apart from others of the same age-group for special teaching all the time.

Representative governors   In voluntary schools, governors not appointed by the Foundation. May be used to indicate those who are elected to represent, e.g. parents.

Residential school   A school at which children with special needs live and are taught. Boarding school is the term for a school which ordinary children attend.

Rising fives Children admitted to a school a term earlier than is required by law.

Role play Method of learning by acting out a situation and assuming a personality.

Rote learning Memorising word for word, without necessarily understanding the meaning.

Scale posts Teachers' salaries were formerly negotiated by the Burnham Committee, which was abolished. *see* Main grade.

School phobia Intense negative feelings sometimes accompanied by physical symptons such as dizziness, nausea, sickness, headache, stomach pains, etc leading to an inability to attend school. Sometimes called school refusal, and not to be confused with truancy.

School private fund Private funds maintained by schools for the furtherance of school activities which are not part of the provision made by the LEA. Should not be used for purchasing essential items such as textbooks and basic materials.

School psychological service *see* Child guidance clinic

Secondary school Catering for pupils from 11 or 12 to 16+.

Secondment A temporary attachment to another school or post for a teacher, or a special course in another institution.

Selective school A grammar school or city technology college, or school accepting pupils under the assisted places scheme.

Setting Placing children in different groups for a particular subject according to their ability in that subject only.

Sin bin Coloquial name for special unit for disruptive pupils.

Sixth-form college A separate school for sixth-form work only. May cater for all young people over 16 from an area, or may be limited to those working for GCE 'A' level examinations.

Sixteen-plus examinations *see* GCSE.

Social and life skills Abilities needed to communicate effectively, manage daily living, and develop meaningful relationships.

Social education Includes personal relationships, communication, health education, sex education, and understanding of the community and the environment.

Special agreement school *see* Voluntary school

Special education For children with sensory, physical, mental, medical or behavioural and emotional difficulties, or a combination of these, who have difficulty in learning.

Special educational needs Roughly two per cent of children have sensory, physical, mental, medical or behavioural and emotional difficulties or a combination of these, requiring a 'statement of special educational needs' under the 1981 Education Act. A further twenty per cent may have a learning difficulty not requiring a statement, but additional help from teachers.

Special school   A school specialising in catering for the needs and education of a specific disability or combination of disabilities.

Special unit   Increasingly, as legislated for in the 1981 Education Act, there is integration of children with disabilities into ordinary schools. In some cases these are catered for in units attached to the school, and integration may take place to a greater or lesser extent.

Specific learning difficulty   Problem with one area of the curriculum, usually reading, writing and/or numeracy. Preferred term to dyslexia for specific reading difficulty.

Split-site school   A school which operates with buildings on more than one site.

Standard number   The number of pupils which the school admitted in 1979, or the number later agreed to be the standard number.

Standardised test   A test which has been tried out and evaluated, and for which there are established norms.

Statement of special educational needs   Written description of a child's educational needs required to be made by an LEA, incorporating advice from teachers, educational psychologists, doctors, parents, professionals and others. Introduced by the Education Act 1981. The process of producing this is called 'statementing'.

Streaming   Grouping of children into different classes for all or most of their work, according to their ability as determined by general attainment (usually in English and/or maths) or general ability tests.

Supply teacher   Temporary substitute teacher for those away through illness, etc.

Syllabus   Course of study in a given subject, often connected with an examination.

Teachers' associations   The largest of the teachers' organisations is the National Union of Teachers, followed by the National Association of Schoolmaster/Union of Women Teachers and Assistant Masters and Mistresses Association and the Professional Association of Teachers. Heads and deputies may also belong to the National Association of Headteachers or Secondary Heads Association.

Teachers' centre   A building provided by the LEA for the in-service training of teachers.

Teaching medium   Language through which subjects are communicated to pupils by teachers. In many schools in Wales the medium will be Welsh.

Teaching practice   Time spent by a student teacher in a school gaining practical teaching experience.

Team teaching   A method of organising teaching in one or a group of subjects, using a number of teachers, and various methods of work, from large-group lectures to small-group work, each teacher contributing to the team plan.

Tertiary college   Combines sixth-form and further education provision. May be full-time or part-time. May include adult education.

Tertiary education   Post-sixteen education. Sometimes limited to education for the 16–19 age-group, sometimes includes adult education.

Testing   Attainment targets will be established for national curriculum subjects, and testing will be carried out at 7, 11, 14, 16 as a result of the 1988 Education Reform Act.

Tutorial   A teacher working on a one-to-one basis with a student or a small group.

TVEI   Technical and Vocational Educational Initiative. Specialised vocational and technical education for the 14–18 age group, intended for a wide range of ability. Financed by the Training Commisssion.

Unit   Some schools have units to cater for truanting, disruptive or emotionally disturbed pupils on site. Other units away from the school are off-site. A variety of titles are given to such units, e.g. sanctuary, withdrawal, secondary tutorial, sin bin, etc. *see also* Special unit

Verbal reasoning test   A test where the emphasis is placed on the ability to understand written and spoken language. May be used for eleven-plus tests.

Vernon spelling test   Administered to first-year juniors (aged 7). Gives teachers a view of the spelling strategies used by individual children.

Vertical grouping   Classes formed (in primary schools) with children of different ages. Also called family grouping.

Virement   System whereby it is permissible to transfer a proportion of money allocated from one heading to another heading in the financial budget.

Vocational education   Studies aimed at training a student for a particular job or career.

Voluntary school There are three main kinds – 'controlled', 'aided' and 'special agreement'. Originally built by voluntary bodies, usually churches, but sometimes trusts. Now largely financed by LEA, though the foundation retains a measure of control. The foundation governors retain a majority over all other interests in aided schools.

Walsall screening Tests administered to children in reception classes. Gives a broad picture of the way the child functions socially, physically and intellectually.

Warnock report The *Special Educational Needs* report produced in 1978 by the committee chaired by Mary Warnock which resulted in the Education Act 1981.

Whole-school approach A planned policy encompassing equal opportunities, careers, homework, applied through the school. Also a method of meeting special educational needs in an ordinary school by exploiting the resources already existing in the school.

Withdrawal class Taking children out of an ordinary class to meet their special needs in various subjects. Extra help is usually given in small groups by a remedial teacher.

Work cards Information sheets on single topics, usually prepared by individual teachers.

Work experience Opportunity provided by arrangement with local firms for pupils to spend some time in a place of work.

Index

Compiled by Elizabeth Wallis